MW01014059

# THE *Spirituality* OF MAZES & LABYRINTHS

Entrance Stone Newgrange, UK

GAILAND MACQUEEN

# THE *Spirituality* OF MAZES & LABYRINTHS

Northstone

CREDITS: page 127

**Library and Archives Canada**
**Cataloguing in Publication**

MacQueen, Gailand, 1937–
The spirituality of mazes & labyrinths/
Gailand MacQueen.
Includes bibliographical references.
ISBN 1-896836-69-0
1. Labyrinths. 2. Maze puzzles.
3. Spiritual life. I. Title.
BL325.L3M34 2005 203'.7
C2005-900196-8

Northstone

An imprint of WOOD LAKE BOOKS, INC.
Kelowna, BC, Canada

www.northstone.com

Printed in Canada at Friesens, Altona, MB

9 8 7 6 5 4 3 2 1

# Contents

Herb Garden

# Acknowledgments

I am grateful to Huntington University in Sudbury, Ontario, and to Manitou Conference of the United Church of Canada for financial assistance for research in England.

The whole team at Northstone Publishing have been invariably kind in their comments, generous with their time, and creative. I have to single out a few members of the team for special thanks. My enthusiasm for mazes and labyrinths was affirmed by Lois Huey Heck's matching enthusiasm for the project. Beth Griffin literally rescued the book when my text vanished into electronic limbo, never to be seen again. Verena Velten turned my rough and shaky sketches into beautiful drawings. Mike Schwartzentruber edited with sensitivity and Margaret Kyle created a setting that allows the story of the maze and the labyrinth to glow. This book is a reflection of their talent. I had thought I was producing a study guide, but the Northstone team has turned it into the sort of book that is beyond my daydreams. Thank you.

The book and I owe much to Jeff Saward, who generously shared both his time and his encyclopedic knowledge of mazes and labyrinths.

I want to thank my son, Geoff, for his careful critical reading of the original manuscript. No one but I will know how much better the book is because of him.

Finally, there is my wife, Joyce. She is a thoughtful critic and a meticulous proofreader. But most of all it is a joy to share her enthusiasms and to have her share mine. Of course, any errors in fact or phraseology are my own.

– Gailand MacQueen

Stardreaming Labyrinth, New Mexico

Hedge Maze, Longleat, Wiltshire, UK

# 1

# The Mystery of the Labyrinth – The Challenge of the Maze

## Experience

Welcome to an adventure of the spirit.

This book tells the story of labyrinths and mazes as spiritual symbols, but it also provides opportunities for you to explore mazes and labyrinths for yourself.

In this chapter, we explore some of the spiritual dimensions of labyrinths and mazes, beginning with the simplest form of each. In later chapters, we will add complexities and see what effect they have. But we start with a basic labyrinth and maze.

Since you will be using the labyrinths and mazes in this book several times, it is best not to mark the paths permanently. The easiest solution is to make several photocopies of each of the illustrations, which you may then mark up as you see fit. You could also trace the paths with a finger or something pointed, such as a skewer; you might trace the path lightly in pencil and erase it. An elegant solution is to purchase a sheet of clear plastic and a marker that can be wiped off. This allows you to trace the path any number of times without marking the paper.

The labyrinth on page 10 is called a Cretan labyrinth, probably because of its association with ancient Crete. Some scholars prefer the term *classical* for this form of labyrinth. The maze on page 11 is based on the famous hedge maze at Hampton Court Palace, outside of London, England.

As you trace the labyrinth or maze, allow yourself to experience it. Then ask yourself the following questions.

At the bottom of each page are instructions beside the "book maze" symbol shown to the right. Please ignore them until the end of Chapter 5 where they will be explained.

*Go to page 46 or 48*

THE CRETAN LABYRINTH

*Go to page 12 or 47*

How did I feel following the labyrinth/maze?

Did I feel confused?
Was that pleasant or unpleasant?

Did the labyrinth/maze have any immediate symbolic meaning for me?

Now trace each of them a second time.

Did your answers to any of the questions change?

The Hampton Court Maze

*Go to page 9 or 10*

# TO BEGIN WITH

From the moment I first learned about the labyrinth, it fascinated me. So it was only natural that, when the labyrinth became popular again as a spiritual path, I wanted to share my passion with others.

A labyrinth is a winding path that leads you inexorably to a center.

When I began to lead workshops on the labyrinth, I inevitably found that there were a few participants who wanted to share wonderful experiences that they had years ago with mazes, especially hedge mazes. I quickly realized that they were talking about a kind of spiritual experience that was different than the experience of the labyrinth, but no less authentic. I have had a passion for mazes for over half a century, longer than my love affair with the labyrinth, so I began incorporating mazes into some of the workshops that I led. Surprisingly, I found that some people found more spiritual meaning in mazes than in labyrinths. Even more surprisingly, there were people who wanted *both* mazes and labyrinths.

In this book, you will encounter two very different spiritual styles symbolized by the labyrinth and by the maze. You will also be offered many opportunities to play with mazes and labyrinths. Each chapter will begin and end with the invitation to experiment for yourself.

*Go to page 49 or 50*

This chapter briefly describes the labyrinth and the maze as spiritual symbols.

Chapter 2 tells the story of the labyrinth, its origins in the mists of prehistory and its gradual eclipse with the development of the modern world after 1400 CE.

Chapter 3 tells the story of mazes from their origins in the hedge gardens of 15th-century Europe, to their decline into children's toys and midway attractions by the end of the 19th century.

Chapter 4 documents the story of my own growing discovery of labyrinths and mazes as spiritual symbols, and of their increasing meaning in my life.

Chapter 5 examines the resurgence of interest in mazes in recent years and the way in which this renewed interest symbolizes recent spiritual trends.

Chapter 6 examines the recent rebirth of the labyrinth and the strands of spirituality, very different from the maze, that it represents.

Welcome to an adventure of the spirit. Walk the labyrinth with me to find your center; walk mazes with me to express your individuality.

## LABYRINTHS

Labyrinths, very much like the one you explored on page 10, have been around for a very long time. In fact, they have been used outside of formal religion as a ritual object to express spiritual values for at least 3500 years, in countries all over the world, including China, India, the Holy Land, Ireland, Southern Europe, Scandinavia, pre-Columbian North America, and England.

Labyrinths and labyrinthine borders are found all over the world in different historic periods: at Neolithic and Sardinian and Hopi rock art sites, in Hindu temples and Taoist shrines, bordering Minoan frescoes and in Roman mosaics. They can also be found in Roman Catholic and Episcopal cathedrals, in Protestant churches, and in New Age retreat centers. They have been carved into rocks, turf, and wood; engraved in metal; laid out in stones; woven in reeds; set in tiles; painted and drawn. They have been traced with fingers and eyes and drawing implements, walked, run, danced, and crawled on hands and knees. The labyrinth is a nearly universal form and comes as close as we can to an archetype.

An archetype is a symbol that appeals to us at an unconscious level. We don't have to struggle with its meaning intellectually. Its symbolic meaning is somehow ingrained in us, part of our very nature. It may appeal to us without our even understanding why. Until about 1400 CE, people seem to have

*Go to page 12 or 50*

encountered the labyrinth in this way. Many still do.

It is always risky to talk about the meaning of such an archetypal symbol. We know that it must carry a wealth of meaning to appeal to so many different sorts of people over such a long time.

But we can, tentatively, explore some of its meanings if we stay aware that we can never really plumb all of its riches.

The first few times you walk the labyrinth you may have a mild sense of confusion – all the twists and turns can deceive you into thinking that the labyrinth is a confusing path you might get lost in. Very quickly, however, you will discover that you can't get lost, as long as you stay on the path and keep walking. Sooner or later, later in a very large labyrinth, you will come to the center. Mathematicians working in a field called topology, which studies the shapes of things as we twist and stretch them, tell us that the labyrinth is really one of the simplest objects there can be – a simple, single path.

Some people with a passion for the confusion and complexity of mazes have trouble understanding all the fuss about the simple labyrinth. The best gift they can imagine coming from walking a labyrinth would be a mild case of vertigo, appealing only to the sort of young children who spin around in order to get dizzy. They have missed the point. The tens of thousands of people, probably hundreds of thousands by now, who have walked the labyrinth during the past 20 years, to say nothing of the untold numbers who used them in the past, were not looking for confusion and complexity, and they were certainly not looking for vertigo. They were seeking a way to be in touch with eternal truths.

The labyrinth is a symbol of our journey through life. The center may be taken to represent enlightenment, self-realization, perfection, or salvation. In medieval France, the center was called "heaven" and the path itself was known as "the way to Jerusalem," the goal of the pilgrim, but also the heavenly city, the goal of all Christians.

As you walk the labyrinth, there will be times when you find yourself tantalizingly close to the goal, but then, suddenly, you find yourself moving away from the center. Likewise, far into the path, you may find yourself on the outer circle. It could be puzzling or even discouraging if you did not know that the entire path is necessary, that the entire path leads to the center – even those parts that seem to lead away from it, even those parts that seem far from it. You can trust the path to take you to the center eventually, no matter where you happen to be at the moment.

Thus, the labyrinth is a powerful symbol of the unity of our life path and of the center that awaits, wherever we are on the path. Alternatively, we might say that the labyrinth is a symbol of God, who is both the center we seek and the path that gets us there. What we need is to trust the center and to trust the path that leads to it.

It is the labyrinth's lack of complexity that allows so many people to use it as a meditative or

*Go to page 13 or 50*

devotional tool. Once we are on the path, our minds are freed from the need to make decisions. We can pray; or focus on our breath, on a mantra, on a scripture passage, or on a problem. We can listen to the wisdom of our bodies, our breath, our steps, our heartbeat. Whether we walk the labyrinth alone or with others, its simplicity offers the possibility that we can clear our minds, cleanse our souls, and celebrate our bodies.

When we walk the labyrinth with others, it becomes a tool for understanding relationships and community. We realize our community with all people. We may be at very different places on the path, but we all share it. We cannot judge anyone because they are moving away from the center or are far from it. Like us, they are on the path toward it. With one turn, those who seem to be almost there may find themselves moving away from it; those who seem to be far away, with one turn may move toward it. We can't even tell where our fellow walkers are on their path in relation to the center. They are one with us and we with them; we are all pilgrims on the same path, with the same hope of reaching the same center.

As well as symbolizing our sense of identification with fellow pilgrims, the labyrinth symbolizes the way that relationships work in life. Sometimes as we walk, we find ourselves walking in the same direction, parallel to another person. Then we encounter a turn and we discover that they are moving away from us; or coming toward us on a different path; or coming toward us on the same path, if they are returning from the center, so that we brush past each other. In the labyrinth, the complex emotional dance of relationships is symbolized in a physical dance of bodies moving through the coils of the path, coming together and moving apart in ever more complex patterns over the simple unity of the path.

From ancient times, the labyrinth has been used in rituals at the most important moments in life. Although we don't always know exactly *how,* its structure, as well as its placement at gravesites, seacoasts, and healing sites, suggests that it was used in rituals associated with birth, coming of age, marriage, sickness, and death, as well as initiation into secret societies or elders' groups.

Like all rites of passage and initiation ceremonies, walking the labyrinth is structured as a pilgrimage with three parts. First comes the journey inward, toward the sacred space where change happens. Next, time is spent at the center, where the new life begins. Finally, there is the journey outward, the return of the transformed person to the world, often with a new identity. Wherever ancient labyrinths are found, people made this pilgrimage.

Today, new labyrinths are being constructed so that people can follow in the footsteps of ancient ancestors in the transitions of their own lives, including new transitions such as divorce and job loss.

*Go to page 11 or 52*

The labyrinth is essentially intuitive; psychologists would call it a right-brain experience. Everything that I have written about the labyrinth so far is a left-brain, rational, intellectual analysis of the intuitive, right-brain experience of walking the labyrinth.

Of course, what I have written is rooted in the work of historians, mathematicians, and modern spiritual thinkers, especially those who have experimented with the labyrinth. For that reason, I hope that you take it seriously, but not too seriously. Your experience is what matters. Trust your own intuition, your own spirituality. What you discover is what you *need* to discover and that is all that really matters as you walk the labyrinth.

## MAZES

Mazes, like the one you explored on page 11, are a relatively recent phenomenon compared to the labyrinth. They were first developed by landscape architects about 600 years ago to satisfy the needs of the newly-rich, land-owning aristocrats and royalty of Europe and Great Britain. They were, possibly, elaborate modifications of hedge labyrinths or, more likely, herbal knot gardens. But the designers brought something radically new into the world – the garden puzzle maze.

Most dictionaries treat the words "labyrinth" and "maze" as synonyms. Both are defined as something like "a tortuous, confusing path, involving many dead ends" – in other words, a puzzle maze. Before the invention of garden mazes, both words referred to what we have been calling "labyrinths." With the rise in the popularity of garden mazes, both words came to refer to puzzle mazes. As interest in the spirituality of the single-path figure increased during the 1980s and 1990s, more and more authors seized on the word "labyrinth" for it, leaving "maze" to refer to the multi-path puzzle. Dictionaries have not yet caught up with this sensible distinction.

It has been easy to confuse the labyrinth with a maze. Looked at from above, it is sometimes difficult to distinguish one from the other. Both are long, twisting paths, contained in a compact shape, leading from an entrance to a center. But here the resemblance stops.

Mathematicians have shown that labyrinths and mazes are not only mathematically distinct, but, in many ways, almost opposites. All labyrinths are topologically identical; in other words, all labyrinths are constituted by a single path leading from entrance to center. Most mazes are topologically unique. Not only are they distinct from labyrinths, they are also different from other mazes. What all mazes share is a network of circularities, switchbacks, dead ends, and other tricks intended to confuse the solver. But

*Go to page 52 or 81*

unless a maze is deliberately copied from another maze, each maze is unique in the permutations of these tricks and the way in which they are used. When you walk a labyrinth, there is a sense in which you have walked all labyrinths; when you solve a maze, you have only solved that particular maze and there remain potentially infinite new maze combinations to puzzle you.

Mazes began as a form of entertainment and they have remained entertainment. They are a pleasant way to while away a few minutes or a few hours when we have nothing else to do. They are a pastime, unconnected with anything important such as religious ritual.

Occasionally, the content of a maze may be religious, especially in children's church school publications. (Can you help Daniel get out of the den without being eaten by lions? Can you help the pilgrim get to Jerusalem without being killed by Saracens?) But this surface subject matter is not essential to the maze; it is purely arbitrary. You could substitute any story without changing the maze. (Can you help the slave escape to Canada without being captured by bounty hunters? Can you help the junior executive climb the corporate ladder without being made redundant?) In fact, you could eliminate Daniel and the pilgrim and the slave and the junior executive, along with the lions and other dangers, and you would still have a perfectly good maze. Most mazes contain no story or content at all; they are just confusing passages and dead ends and a final goal. In mazes where there *is* content or a story, whether or not it is religious, it is layered over the *form* of a maze, which could just as easily stand on its own.

Mazes, as mazes, are not intended for any serious purpose; they are intended for fun and frustration. But this does not mean that mazes have no symbolic spiritual significance. It just means that they are not specifically intended by either their designers or their solvers to be such symbols. They are intended to provide entertainment, a challenge, a mental workout.

When we think about spirituality, the first things we think about are not usually pastimes or entertainment or even mental challenges. We are more likely to think of spirituality in relation to the sacred and to associate it with religion and the transcendent. This is why many people have difficulty recognizing the maze as a spiritual symbol. Mazes contain no overt religious or transcendent content or purpose at all. They appear to be purely secular.

But this is exactly the point. This is what makes the maze such a perfect symbol for the human condition in a period of history which is itself secular; secularity marks the spirit of the modern age, the age when puzzle mazes were invented and rose to popularity.

Many scholars have pointed to the disappearance of the sacred in the modern world. Some people have deplored the loss of the sacred, predict-

*Go to page 84 or 103*

ing a decline in morality and civility. Others have celebrated the loss of the sacred as an opportunity for humanity finally to take full responsibility for its own destiny. However we may feel about this process of secularization, it is the very core of the spirit of the modern world, so any symbol of the modern spirit would have to represent the secular. Mazes have many features that make them powerful as symbols of this modern, secular spirit. Their uncompromising secularity is, perhaps, their most obvious feature.

Secularization requires constant personal choice; many modern people no longer depend on religion or tradition to tell them what they ought to do. Throughout most of history, people had few personal choices. The big things in life were determined by birth or family or religion or tribe. The work a person would do, whom they would marry, and what they would believe were often set before they were born. But this is no longer so. Think about the major decisions in your life. How did you decide what to study? What work to do? Whom to marry? Where to live? How many children to have and when to have them? There was a time not so long ago when the church or the family dictated all of these decisions. Today, you probably decided for yourself, indeed you probably *insisted* on deciding for yourself, and you took responsibility for the consequences of your choices.

In previous times, even day-to-day life was largely circumscribed by family, tradition, and religion. In the modern world, most of us have to make dozens, even hundreds, of decisions every day. And it becomes harder and harder to tell which decisions are life changing and which don't really matter. Just doing the family shopping involves choosing between many products, many brands, many kinds of packaging. In previous times, my Scottish ancestors, for example, were fortunate to have oats. Today I can choose between at least a dozen different grains and decide whether I want them popped or flaked, plain, sugared, honeyed, candied, colored, instant, microwaveable, or ready to eat; bulk or boxed or vacuum-sealed; large, extra-large or family size. Nutritionists tell us that this choice matters a great deal; our children's, and our own, health is at stake.

This is a seemingly trivial example of the constant necessity of making decisions, all too often important decisions, which can change our lives or the lives of other people forever. One reason that I love to fly on commercial airlines is the little vacation that I get from the responsibility of choosing; I say whether I'd prefer beef or chicken (more and more we don't even get that choice) and, for a few hours, someone else takes over. Most of modern life is a maze of decisions in which we have no choice but to choose.

The repeated choices in mazes between turning one way or another may be taken as a symbol of the importance of personal choice in the modern world. Whether we solve the maze, and how long it takes us,

*Go to page 54 or 57*

are results of our decision making. The maze designer sets out to fool us. Whether we are fooled depends on our choices. Our memory, reason, and astuteness all come into play in our attempt not to be fooled. Solving a maze elegantly, by finding the shortest path, is our goal, but we may have to settle for a few dead ends along the way. Solving the maze is a celebration of our decisions and our abilities.

Mazes are essentially competitive. The solver is always in competition with the designer. Often, the solver is in competition with other solvers as well. Who will be the first to reach the treasure at the center of the maze? Even when there are no other players, mazes often have time limits. In all of this, mazes reflect the competitiveness of our society.

One of the major beliefs in the modern world is that the competitive free market should determine the value of products and services. The better products and services will succeed and survive; others will fall by the wayside. However, this metaphor, derived from economics, is applied to everything else in the modern world, from sport to dating to education, even to the value of individual persons. This idea of universal competition is really an attempt to apply Darwin's theory of the survival of the fittest to social relations. Mazes are powerful symbols, then, of the idea of competition, which permeates modern thought, especially modern social theories.

So deeply ingrained is this idea of competition today that it is difficult to imagine any other way of thinking about social relations. But, like the maze that symbolizes it, it is a relatively new idea. Through the long centuries before, social relations were typically characterized by obedience, one alternative to competition. A person's role in life was to be obedient to tradition and to those with authority. Even those in positions of power were under the authority of their traditions.

This idea of obedience is most powerfully expressed in Buddhist and Christian monastic traditions. Other alternative bases for social relationships are justice, as called for by the Hebrew prophets; and love, even love of enemies, as taught by Jesus. All of these alternatives to competition are communal in nature. But competition is individualistic and so is the maze that symbolizes it.

Solving a maze is an individual accomplishment. As I walk a maze, I really have no interest in where other walkers are. They are irrelevant to my path. I am focused on the puzzle and on my decisions. Others, either the maze designer or rival solvers, exist only as challengers. Symbolically, the maze is all about my accomplishments, my decisions, my consequences. "It's all about me," to echo a popular phrase – about my success or failure. In this respect, the maze symbolizes the individualism that is so important to the spirit of the modern world. Most other cultures have tended to be community-oriented. Each person filled a role, which served the needs of the greater community. The elevation

*Go to page 18 or 20*

of self was the ultimate sin – a sin like Satan's, of putting the self above God, above the community, above inherited wisdom. In our world, aggressive individualism is the road to success and the solitariness of the individual in the maze, dependent on his own wits alone to solve the puzzle, represents this perfectly.

Modern life is a maze of complication and confusion. We are constantly bombarded with information, much of it contradictory, much of it trivial, some of it vital, but all of it claiming our attention. Every day we are served up a smorgasbord of political and religious ideas: 20 different versions of right, left, and center; dozens of fundamentalisms and liberalisms and traditionalisms. Every television newscast, newspaper story, and magazine article tries to tell us what to think. But even when they are about the same issue or event, they tell us to believe different things.

Every purported fact and idea and ideology lays its claim upon us. We are confronted with a vast array of cultural choices. More than anything else we need critical awareness, what religions have called discernment, to find our way through this mass of confusion. Mazes represent modern confusion and complication perfectly. Every new turn tempts us. After all, it just might be the one that leads to the pot of gold.

Every maze has a solution, if only we can get it right. Likewise, in our modern world, every phenomenon is thought to have a rational, scientific explanation, if only we can find it. As a result, we have tended to reject irrational explanations of experience and have sought to banish the spirits and the angels, the demons and the ghosts, not to mention the fairies at the bottom of the garden, in the cold light of reason and the hard evidence of science. The fact that the spiritual realm refuses to go away does not deter the modern project from trying to get rid of it. The maze represents this modern rationalizing drive. No matter how difficult or puzzling a maze may be, there has to be a reasonable solution to it.

*Go to page 55 or 57*

# THE SPIRITUAL JOURNEY

It is obvious that the labyrinth symbolizes a spiritual journey closely connected with traditional religion. It is less obvious that mazes *also* symbolize a spiritual journey because they are so clearly not connected with religion of any kind. Yet, as the labyrinth did for its time, mazes almost perfectly symbolize the spirit of the modern world. Where the labyrinth represents simplicity, mazes symbolize complexity and confusion. Where the labyrinth is about trust, mazes are about personal choice. Where the labyrinth is communal, mazes are individualistic. Where the labyrinth strengthens relationships, mazes celebrate competition. Where the labyrinth is an instrument of ritual, mazes are pastimes. Where the labyrinth is intuitive, mazes are rational. Where the labyrinth represents unity, mazes point to diversity. Where the labyrinth is sacred space, mazes are purely secular diversions.

Some people find a sense of accomplishment in solving a maze, which is a reflection of their sense of accomplishment in their successes in life. They are uncomfortable with the idea of trusting the single path of the labyrinth. Others do not like the complex, competitive picture that mazes give of the spirit of the modern world. They need the simple spirituality that the labyrinth can offer. But these people would be unwise to ignore the message that mazes give us. No one is untouched by the spirit of the modern world. Still other people want the choice of spiritual styles. It is said that, in ancient China, people were Confucians at work and Taoists at home. There are some people who appreciate differing spiritual symbols, such as the labyrinth and the maze, appropriate to their different life experiences.

CHILDREN WALKING A MAZE, PARHAM, SUSSEX, UK

*Go to page 20 or 54*

## Embodied Spirituality

When I was a child in the 1940s, little boys were very quickly categorized. There were the jocks; they could catch a ball and run fast. There were the "artsies"; they could carry a tune and draw a pig. Then there were people like me; we could think. We couldn't dance and we couldn't sing; our handwriting was abominable; but boy could we think. Once we had been categorized as thinkers, teachers pressured us to find our meaning within our minds and discouraged all-round development. At one level, I really appreciate what this sort of education did for me. It has given me a wonderful life as a university professor. At another level, I deeply resent it. I have spent most of my life trying to recapture my feelings and my body. This is a personal spiritual issue, not a professional one.

For years and years, I was only aware of feelings when they became extreme. I used to go away to workshops to get in touch with my subtler feelings. Two weeks, later I'd be back in my head again. Slowly, slowly, I began to get in touch with my emotional life. At last, my subtle feeling-changes from moment to moment became real to me.

Eventually I met Alexandra Caverley Lowery, a wonderful spiritual director who helped me to get in touch with the spirituality of my body. She helped me to express my faith and my doubts, my hopes and my fears, through movement. She gave me permission to whisper and dance, to shout and bark like a dog, to weep and laugh and jump for joy.

At the same time that I was working with Alexandra, I encountered the Dances for Sacred Peace, a Jewish Kabbalistic interpretation of the Moslem Sufi dervish tradition, led by a Protestant minister. This was another form of embodied spirituality, another way of saying that the body is sacred, too. In the rhythm of many bodies moving in unison to ancient chants, I found a sense of the unity of faith and a feeling of the presence of the Spirit. I had been taught that my mind was what really mattered; I was learning that my body matters, too, at least when it comes to worship.

We have always known at one level that our bodies need to worship as much as our minds do. We fold our hands and bow our heads for grace. We cross ourselves. We kneel for prayer. Yet modern Western people, especially Protestants, perhaps most especially male Protestants, have trouble trusting their bodies as spiritual vehicles.

Labyrinths and mazes are about embodiment. When we wander a hedge maze, or when we walk, run, or crawl the labyrinth, we are using our bodies. Our spirituality becomes embodied even when we trace labyrinths and mazes with a finger, or dance through the pathways in our imagination. Labyrinths and mazes help us to rediscover our bodies as vehicles of spirituality.

*Go to page 21 or 55*

## EXPERIENCE

You may have found a lot of left-brain information packed into this chapter. Return to the labyrinth on page 10 and the maze on page 11. Use your intuition as you follow the labyrinth, and your reason as you figure out the maze. How does this affect your experience of the labyrinth and maze? How does the information you found in this chapter change the experience of tracing the labyrinth or the maze? Ask yourself questions similar to those you asked at the beginning of the chapter.

- How did I feel while I followed the labyrinth/maze?
- Did I feel confused?
- Was it pleasant or unpleasant?
- What, if any, new symbolic meaning did the labyrinth/maze take on for me?
- Did I gain any new insights from this labyrinth/maze experience?
- If so, what were they?

Are there any large-scale labyrinths or mazes that you could walk near where you live? Many churches and denominational and New Age retreat centers have labyrinths, which they share with the public. Even if they don't have one, these churches and retreat centers may be able to tell you where to find a labyrinth nearby. Failing this, if you have access to the Internet, go to http://wwll.veriditas.labyrinthsociety.org which is the WorldWide Labyrinth Locator.

You may have more difficulty locating a large-scale maze. There are Internet sites that give maze locations, but most of these sites are British or European, so their coverage of North American maze locations is a bit weak. A 1995 CD-ROM called MAZE (see the resource list at the end of the book) has an extensive list of important maze sites all over the world, but it is dated and only covers selected sites. MAZE also includes a virtual walk of a variety of mazes of differing levels of difficulty. The simulation is quite effective: not as powerful as a walk-through maze, but certainly a good second best.

Sometimes one can find a maze through sheer luck. Driving on Manitoulin Island, in Ontario, I came across a sign for a hedge maze in the tiny village of Kagawong. Someone there has built a delightful little cedar maze, which is free and always open. Farmers sometimes supplement their income by cutting mazes into grain fields, especially cornfields, sort of maize mazes. Once you start looking for mazes and labyrinths, it is amazing how often they will come to you.

You can also find a variety of role-playing games on CD-ROM that involve interesting maze simulations, but you will probably have to kill someone or something around every corner in order to follow the maze.

*Go to page 24 or 58*

If all else fails, Adrian Fisher and Howard Loxton's book *Secrets of the Maze* (see the resource list at the end of the book) contains a "maze simulator," which can be used to prevent you from seeing what is ahead, thus creating something of the experience of a real maze. However, the maze is still flat and on paper.

Enjoy walking or running or dancing the large scale labyrinth/maze, or mousing your way through the computer simulation, or using your simulator to trace a drawing of a maze. Then ask yourself the same questions:

- How did I feel while I followed the labyrinth/maze?
- Did I feel confused? Was it pleasant or unpleasant?
- What, if any, new symbolic meaning did the labyrinth/maze take on for me?
- Did I gain any new insights from this labyrinth/maze experience? If so, what were they?

You might also want to ask yourself how the experience compared to tracing a labyrinth/maze on paper.

*Go to page 59 or 60*

# 2

# The Story of the Labyrinth

## EXPERIENCE

The labyrinth has a beautiful form. It appears to be very complex, especially as we add more and more rings to it. You might suppose that it is very difficult to draw and in some forms it is. But it is possible to draw a beautiful and complex Cretan labyrinth freehand by following a few simple steps. There is real satisfaction in seeing the complex pattern opening up, as you draw a few lines on a blank page. You also gain a different type of insight from the experience of creating your own labyrinth.

This experience begins with an invitation to draw the simplest possible Cretan labyrinth, then goes on to show how to draw labyrinths of any degree of complexity.

*Go to page 24 or 59*

***Drawing the three-ringed labyrinth***

**Step 1:**
Draw a cross and place four dots, as in the diagram.

**Step 2:**
Connect the top of the vertical line of the cross to the dot to its right.

**Step 3:**
Connect the dot at the top left of the vertical line to the right end of the horizontal line.

**Step 4:**
Connect the left end of the horizontal line to the dot in the lower right-hand corner.

**Step 5:**
Connect the lower left-hand dot to the bottom of the vertical line.

You have completed a three-ringed labyrinth.

*Go to page 60 or 87*

If you instinctively drew all the curves in a clockwise direction, as most people do, you might like to see what it is like to draw it in a more counterintuitive way, by drawing them in a counterclockwise direction, as in the diagram below.

If you instinctively drew them in a counterclockwise direction, try clockwise as in the diagram on the right. How does it feel to reverse the direction you naturally would use for drawing?

Counterclockwise

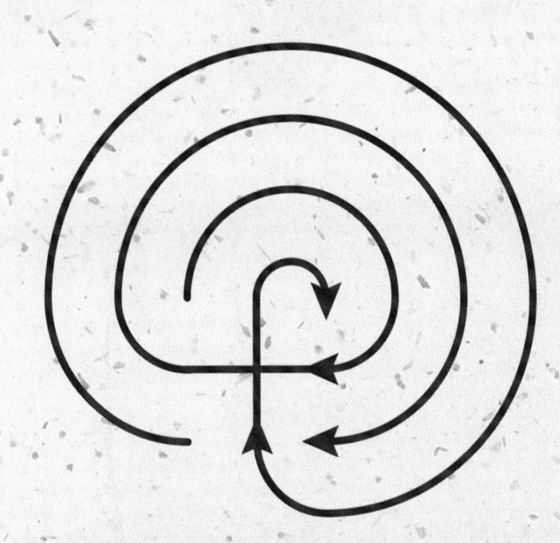

Clockwise

Now that you understand the principles of drawing Cretan labyrinths, it is possible to draw labyrinths of any possible size. All you need is a starting point. For this, simply inject right angles between the cross and the dots.

*Go to page 28 or 63*

***Drawing the seven-ringed labyrinth:***

**Step 1:**
Begin in the same way as for the three-ringed labyrinth, except that a right angle is inserted between each of the dots and the cross.

**Step 2:**
Connect the top of the vertical line of the cross to the top of the right angle next to it.

**Steps 3–9:**
Continue adding parallel curves as in the three-ringed labyrinth.

*Go to page 29 or 64*

Once again, you might find it interesting to draw this larger labyrinth in a counterintuitive way and ask yourself how this experience differs from drawing it in a way that feels more natural.

You will have noticed that there is a way to draw a three-ringed and a seven-ringed labyrinth, but a four-, five-, or six-ringed symmetrical labyrinth is not possible. This is a general principle. The smallest possible number of rings is three and the possible number of rings increases in increments of four. Thus three, seven, 11, 15, 19, 23, etc. rings are possible, but four, five, six, eight, nine, ten, 12, etc. are not. This is true not just of Cretan labyrinths, but of all symmetrical labyrinths. The British turf labyrinths and European cathedral labyrinths that we will encounter in this chapter, which have quite different patterns from Cretan labyrinths, are usually still limited to three, seven, 11, etc. rings.

ON THE WALL OF A 15TH-CENTURY CHURCH, RATHMORE, UK

For those who may already have become addicted to drawing labyrinths (it happens easily), I have provided the first step for the 11-ringed labyrinth and for the 27-ringed labyrinth below.

HOW TO START AN 11-RINGED LABYRINTH

HOW TO START A 27-RINGED LABYRINTH

*Go to page 63 or 64*

# To Begin With

We are entering the ancient world of labyrinths. Walk gently; walk with respect; remove your shoes. The ancients touched the earth with their bare feet and it behooves us to do the same. And yet we are not ancient peoples.

We begin somewhere else, for what we know of modern science affects what we know of ancient wisdom. So we carry our modern sensibility into the ancient Neolithic world. "Turning and turning in the widening gyre…"

The Neolithic Spiral

***Spirals***

It all began somewhere back then: art and science and even spirituality. Somewhere, tens of thousands of years ago someone carved the first decorative spiral, perhaps on mammoth ivory and things began to change. Six millennia ago people began to carve them at gravesites such as Newgrange in Ireland. Some ancient ancestor must have believed that the spirals would somehow guide the dead to new life, either moving to the center toward some sort of heaven, or moving outward toward rebirth and reincarnation. We can never know. But we *do* know that an era had begun.

*Go to page 29 or 31*

Newgrange is not the only site where spirals decorate graves. Such sites can be found in Europe, Africa, Asia, and North America. Wherever people struggled with the meaning of death, spirals appeared.

We can't help but wonder how much our ancient ancestors knew. We know now that the spiral is the basis of all life, perhaps the basis of everything. Scientists today are studying the spiral pattern of water running down drains, of leaves on plants, of seeds within flowers, of genes in DNA molecules, of stars in nebulae. Wherever we look, the spiral organizes atoms into matter, matter into life, life into thought. Our ancient ancestors could not have known about that. Or could they? Could some vague instinct, some intuition that this was what mattered, have led them to carve spirals into the graves of those who meant the most to them?

It's a small step from the spiral to the labyrinth. Some people speculate that a rock spiral cracked and slid one path down forming a proto-labyrinth. I prefer to believe that 5000 or so years ago some uncelebrated genius recognized a different way of drawing a spiral, which said something new and important to her or him. Whatever really happened, the labyrinth was born and it became a favorite subject of rock artists.

***The Labyrinth, the Monster, and the Double-Headed Axe***

Our word labyrinth is derived from the Greek word for the Cretan labyrinth. A common misconception is that it comes from *labrys,* supposedly an ancient Minoan word for double-headed axe. We know that these axes were ritual objects, because they were made of soft bronze and couldn't possibly be used to cut anything; also, such axes were sometimes used to decorate bull sculptures, both in Asia Minor and at Knossos. It seems that the axe was used in the worship of Zeus as a white bull. And that leads us into the myth of the first labyrinth. I will tell the story as though it is history and then search for its meanings, ancient and modern.

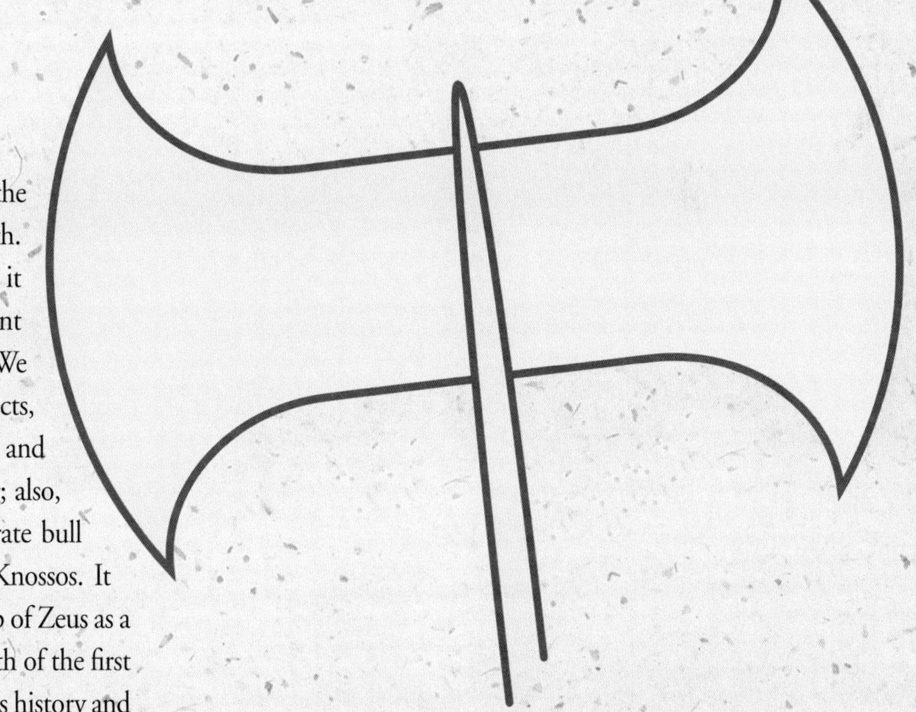

THE DOUBLE-HEADED AXE

*Go to page 29 or 90*

Zeus, who would become the king of the Greek pantheon of gods, was born in a cave high up in the mountains of the Aegean island that today is called Crete. Like so many mythological figures, his survival was a miracle. His mother saved him from his father Chronos, who normally ate his children. When he grew to virile adult godhood, Zeus had many lovers, both human and divine. One such was Europa, whom he approached in the guise of a white bull and carried off to Crete on his back. There she bore him three sons, who founded the three great cities of Crete. The most important of these sons was Minos, who founded Knossos on the north side of the island near the modern city of Herakleion.

At Knossos, Zeus was worshipped in the form of a beautiful, sacred white bull. The Athenian inventor Daedalus, who was living in exile at Knossos, made a wooden heifer so that Pasiphae, Minos' wife, could couple with the bull. She probably did this in revenge for Minos' many infidelities. Whatever her motives, she gave birth to a terrible creature, a bloodthirsty monster with the body of a powerful man and the head of a bull. Minos locked this Minotaur in the labyrinth, another of Daedalus' inventions.

OTFRID LABYRINTH

At this time, Minos demanded tribute from Athens, because he held the Athenians responsible for the death of one of his sons. Every nine years, seven youths and seven maidens were sent to Knossos to be given to the Minotaur. On one of these expeditions, the hero Theseus replaced one of the youths. When they arrived at Knossos, Minos' daughter Ariadne fell in love with Theseus and gave him a magic ball of twine, another of Daedalus' inventions. Theseus entered the labyrinth, fought and killed the Minotaur, and followed the twine back to safety. Theseus and Ariadne fled from Crete, and, in most modern stories, would have lived happily ever after – but not in Greek myth. Somehow, Theseus managed to leave Ariadne behind, sleeping on the isle of Naxos, where she married the god Dionysus and apparently led a reasonably happy life. Theseus, on the other hand, succeeded to the throne of Athens. His reign was a particularly bloody one; he unified the city and created a federation of Greek cities by killing large numbers of opponents. Theseus chose the head of a bull as a symbol of his reign and had it cast on his coinage.

Minoan Bull Fresco

Back at Knossos, Minos was furious with Daedalus. He certainly had enough reasons: his wife had betrayed him with a bull; his daughter had been carried off and then abandoned; and his authority over Athens had been destroyed. As punishment, Minos threw Daedalus and his son Icarus into the very labyrinth that Daedalus had invented. They escaped using another of Daedalus' inventions, feather wings attached to their shoulders by wax. Even this part of the story ended tragically when Icarus flew too close to the sun and the wax melted, plunging him into the sea.

Through the myth of Theseus and the Minotaur, the Athenians explained how the brave mainlanders achieved ascendancy over the Minoans in controlling the commerce of the western Mediterranean. It has everything to foster national pride: a corrupt enemy with an evil monster as its champion, a flawed but brave and handsome hero, a touching side plot about a doomed love, and an explanation of the origin of Athens' political institutions. We still read and love the story. Of course, we recognize that it is myth not history; even most ancient Greeks probably recognized that. But myth is rooted in history, isn't it? Must not something like the story – minus monsters and magic string and flying too near the sun –have happened? Otherwise, wouldn't

*Go to page 32 or 66*

Crete still dominate commerce from North Africa to mainland Greece?

The archeological and historical evidence tells quite a different story of the fall of Knossos. A great maritime culture developed on Crete prior to 1700 BCE. These Minoans traded with Egypt, the Middle East, and mainland Greece. About 1700 BCE, Crete was devastated by an earthquake. New palaces were built on the sites of the old, the most important of these being Knossos, which was really a great commercial center housed in one vast building. The art and jewelry of the Minoans is fresh and modern-looking even today. There is no evidence of human sacrifice at Knossos and almost none anywhere on Crete. The residue in their huge jars is oil, wine, and grain – unlike such jars from the same time period at Carthage and in the Middle East, which were often full of human bones. The Minoans appear to have been a relatively peaceful people considering the times, nor is there any evidence of the Athenians or anyone else conquering the Minoans before 1530 BCE, when Minoan power suddenly collapsed.

What really happened is that the nearby island of Santorini erupted sometime around 1530 BCE (some archeologists date the eruption a century earlier). This was a huge volcanic event that sent a vast tidal wave and a blanket of ash over Crete. The subsequent earthquake shattered the huge palaces. We can only imagine that most of the Minoan fleet was wrecked, and, in any event, Minoan civilization never recovered.

Was there really a labyrinth at Knossos? Some scholars believe that it was only a secure prison. Others believe that the labyrinth was a pattern in the stone floor of a sacred forum, where bull worship was carried out; the worshippers, they say, danced the pattern while leaping the actual bull. One of the frescoes at Knossos shows two youths and a maiden performing just such a ritual, though the floor is not shown. Certainly, labyrinthine patterns border some of the frescoes at Knossos and a thousand years later the earliest Cretan coins display the seven-ringed labyrinth. Whether or not there was an actual labyrinth at ancient Knossos (and I am increasingly convinced that there was), this is where our story of the labyrinth begins.

CRETAN COINS

At a psychological level, the myth of Theseus and the Minotaur has always represented the victory of our rational, civilized self over our animal instincts. Freud would have described it as the victory of the reality principle over the pleasure principle. Today, we would be more likely to describe it as the victory of the frontal lobes of our brain over our reptile brain. However

*Go to page 32, 36 or 65*

we wish to describe it, we are talking about something that is necessary for civilization and culture to develop. Theseus and the Minotaur are not two independent beings in this interpretation. They are two facets of every human being. If we are to survive, it is essential that our reasoning, moral self plunge deep into our inner darkness to slay the beast that dwells there. Though most religions would not put it in such violent terms, they all call on us to endure some sort of "dark night of the soul" and in the process dismiss the false ego that prevents our enlightenment. In that sense, the myth of Theseus, the Minotaur, and the dark path of the labyrinth is as fresh and meaningful today as it ever was.

## A World of Labyrinths

The labyrinth caught on, from Neolithic art sites, to Cretan coins, to Roman mosaics. The Romans sometimes used the labyrinth for rituals but they also loved decorative mosaic floor labyrinths, especially if you could show Theseus at the center, with a huge club in one hand and the severed head of the Minotaur in the other.

The Romans also weren't much for circles. Most of their labyrinths were made up of straight paths and right angles. But they *did* create mosaic labyrinth floors all over the Empire.

A Roman Labyrinth Mosaic

*Go to page 68 or 93*

Labyrinths have had an appeal to varying cultures all over the world. This makes it almost impossible to believe that it somehow "spread" such distances. Rather, it seems easier to believe (for me at least) that the labyrinth is a true archetype; that, somehow, the human spirit had evolved to the point where, everywhere and all at once, it needed the labyrinth to express itself.

SCANDINAVIAN STONE LABYRINTH, TISVILDELEJE, DENMARK

In Chapter 4, we will explore the Rocky Valley labyrinths in Cornwall. It is barely possible to imagine some stranded Phoenician sailor, who had brief contact with Crete, carving them into the rock. The rock labyrinths of Scandinavia stretch the imagination to its limits. The woven labyrinths of the Pima and the carved Hopi labyrinths in Arizona blow it away completely.

On shorelines in Scandinavia there are labyrinths made of rocks. Sailors would walk these labyrinths before a sea voyage in the hope that the winds would be fair. This is part of an ancient spiritual tradition rooted in the idea that symbolic objects or actions can affect what happens in the real world. People believed that real events can be affected by symbolic actions. I could spit, or cross my fingers, or knock wood to avoid calamity. I could light a candle to carry my prayers upward. If I were more modern, I could wear my lucky suit or carry a rabbit's foot. Or, I might just say my mantra before I got on the plane. This is not

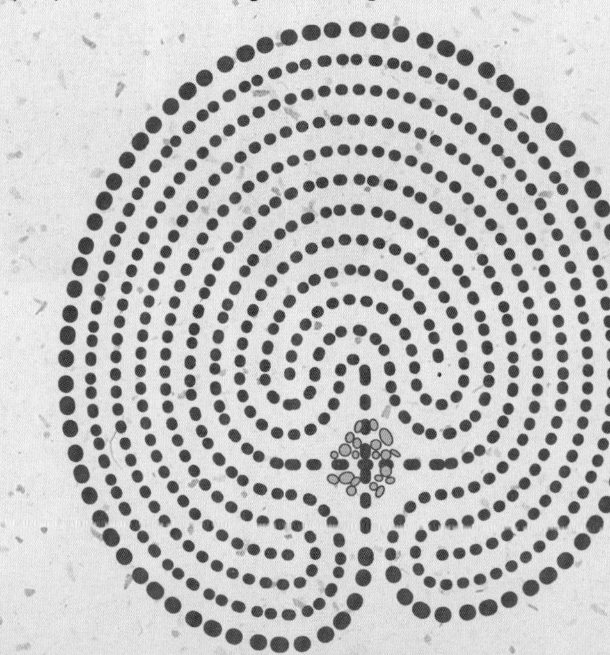

*Go to page 35 or 94*

The Form of a
Pima Woven Labyrinth

just superstition; it is human psychology. This idea of the effectiveness of magical objects and actions may have no basis in science, but it has a profound basis deep in the mind. Probably, we all unconsciously use objects or actions in this way sometimes. In the Scandinavian labyrinths, the practice rose to consciousness to give the sailors assurance.

On Anderson Lake in Northern Ontario, ten minutes south of the Trans-Canada Highway, there is a Native, Roman Catholic spiritual center. One of its features is a labyrinth made of birch logs laid out in a seven-ringed pattern on grass. It is identified in the center's literature as a Hopi labyrinth and its pattern is identical to the seven-ringed Cretan labyrinth.

A number of tribes in the southwestern United States used labyrinths. In the Pima tradition, the legendary hero Siuku escaped from evil pursuers by walking labyrinthine paths that they could not follow. A labyrinth carved on a building abandoned before the arrival of Europeans may be of more recent origin but the pre-Columbian Nasca lines in Peru contain spirals and labarinthine shapes. When the labyrinth was woven into baskets and other objects by the Pima, the shape of the paths was transformed because of the medium, but the actual topological form remains identical to the seven-ringed Cretan labyrinth. The presence of labyrinths in pre-contact North and South America strongly suggests that it is something more than merely a cultural phenomenon; it suggests that the labyrinth is a true archetype to which all people respond instinctively.

In England, the labyrinth is a symbol of pre-Christian spirituality. It is found in many forms, but primarily as the turf "maze" used in modern reworking of ancient fertility rituals. Though these were often *called* mazes, they were invariably labyrinths. The English labyrinth had many names: mizmaze, Julian's

*Go to page 32 or 69*

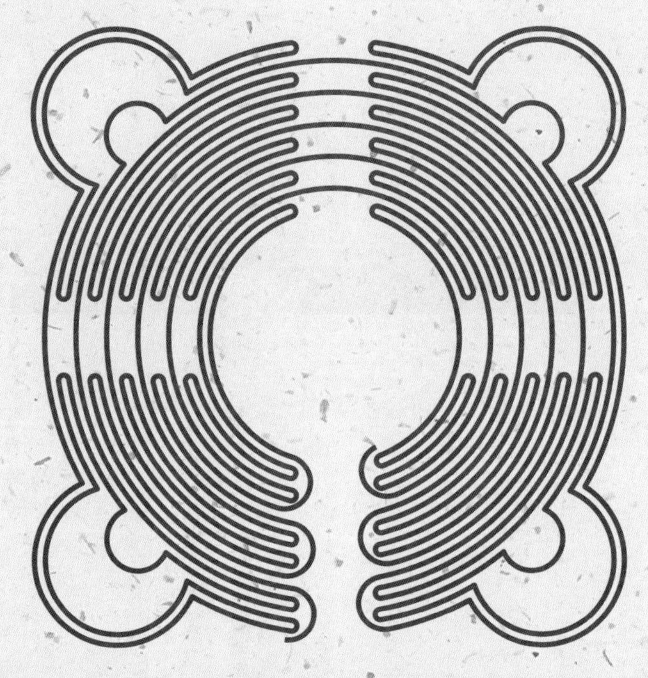

The Saffron Walden Turf Labyrinth

Bower, Troy Town, and Robin Hood's Race. Most of these names refer to rustic practices: young men racing for prizes of girls standing at the center or, more often, for prizes of beer; mistresses hidden away in bowers from jealous wives; sanctuary from guilt. The Welsh word for labyrinth is *Caerdroia,* city of Troy, which is probably a corruption of *caer y troiae,* city of turning. The word is still used today in the title of the most important labyrinth journal, *Caerdroia.*

The labyrinth at Saffron Walden is typical of English turf labyrinths. Mystery surrounds its origins, but we know it was re-cut in the 17th century. With 17 rings and a path over a mile long, it may well be the largest of the surviving ancient labyrinths. Another typical example is Julian's Bower, an 11-ringed turf labyrinth at Alkborough. The pattern these two labyrinths share, which is that of English turf labyrinths in general, represents a radical departure from the Cretan labyrinth – the pattern of turns is quite complex and the path sometimes actually wraps around a large central area. These labyrinths also feature a series of axe shapes along their major axes: 14 axes in the labyrinth at Saffron Walden, nine in Julian's Bower. These axes have become significant recently for people who use labyrinths for spiritual purposes and will be discussed in a later chapter. This pattern was similar to many of the European cathedral labyrinths in the 13th and 14th centuries.

*Go to page 37 or 71*

On midsummer's morn or at the dawn of the spring equinox, the turf labyrinths would be walked or run or more probably danced to ensure a good crop. Barren women may have slept at the center of these labyrinths at the full moon to ensure pregnancy, as they did with ancient chalk hill figures, such as the Cerne Abbas Giant, near Dorset. It is probable that the Puritans, from Elizabethan times on, classified them with Maypoles and mince pies as dangerous pagan superstition.

## MEDIEVAL CHRISTIAN LABYRINTHS

There are examples of labyrinths in churches as far back as the fourth century CE. There is, for example, a square labyrinth at the Church of Reparatus at Orleansville, in Algeria. It looks exactly like a Roman pavement labyrinth except that it has the words *sancta eclesia* embedded in its center as a magic square, reading the same in all directions, to give it a holy meaning. Several churches in Italy included labyrinths of various sizes and patterns. So the pagan labyrinth, like so many other pagan symbols and practices, had somehow been integrated into the Christian church.

Then, in the early 13th century, a dramatic new kind of cathedral came into being, especially in France. Two architectural discoveries, the exterior flying buttress and the interior Gothic arch, made it possible to create buildings that towered over everything around them and that allowed light to pour in through huge glass windows between slender stone pillars. These cathedrals have been described as frozen music. Some research suggests that it was not just the size or the amazing light that uplifted the spirit in the Gothic cathedral, it was the architecture itself. There is something in the very proportions of the building that inclines the soul to the spiritual (perhaps even something in their location on very ancient sacred sites). This mysterious "something" that so enraptures the soul has come to be known as sacred geometry. One feature of this architecture was the

*Go to page 37 or 70*

The Chartres Labyrinth

*Go to page 38 or 71*

labyrinth laid in stone on the floor of the building. Many of these labyrinths have been destroyed, but enough examples remain to give us some understanding of their role.

The Chartres labyrinth near Paris, France, is the largest existing cathedral labyrinth and a typical example. It is 42.3 feet in diameter, almost the same size as the magnificent rose window in the west wall above it. The labyrinth could be a shadow of the window on the cathedral floor. At its center is an abstract floral shape representing a rose. The rose has often been used as a symbol of both Mary and Jesus Christ. (We still sing *Lo, How a Rose E'er Blooming* at Christmas.) Around the outside of the labyrinth are 112 small concave shapes; these are unique to the Chartres labyrinth. The length of the path is 286 or 287 yards so it was sometimes called "the league," which in ancient France was 1500 paces. Labyrinths were also called "meanders," for obvious reasons.

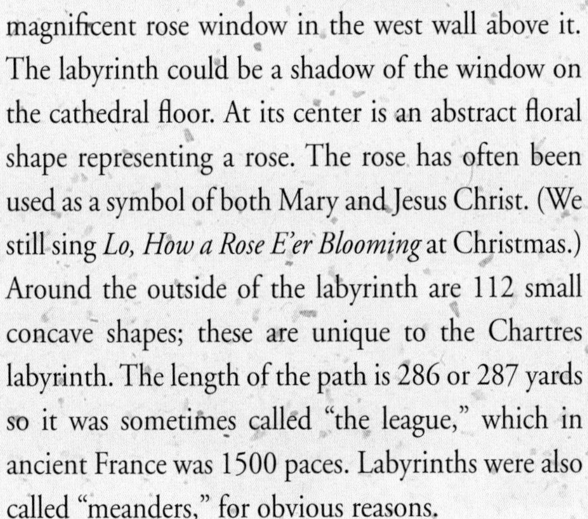

The cathedral labyrinth was sometimes called "the road to Jerusalem" and its center "Jerusalem." These cathedrals were built during the age of pilgrimage. Depending on their circumstances, medieval people traveled to Canterbury, in England; to Santiago, in Spain; to Rome; and especially to Jerusalem. Pilgrimage, especially pilgrimage to the Holy Land, offered the faithful a special blessing. People went for many reasons: devotion, penance, or just a wish to see the world beyond their own town. But not everyone could go on pilgrimage. Some people didn't have the money; some didn't have the time; some didn't have the necessary stamina. For them, the cathedral labyrinth offered a mini pilgrimage, their own symbolic journey to Jerusalem. We can imagine that people walked or ran or crawled the labyrinth, as they did the last steps of a geographical pilgrimage, receiving somewhat the same benefits that all pilgrims received: forgiveness, hope, and grace. In the same vein, the centers of cathedral labyrinths were often called *ciel,* which means heaven. So it was not just Jerusalem, the earthly city of God, that they were pursuing, but the heavenly city, the new Jerusalem.

Cathedral labyrinths were also known as *daedale.* They symbolized the creative spirit of Daedalus, who was not only the inventor of the labyrinth, but also the creator of the builder's tools and the first architect. The labyrinth became a way in which the anonymous architects could put their personal stamp

*Go to page 39 or 72*

on their creations, often with a metal plaque at the center, which would include their mark or their initials along with some symbol of the defeat of the Minotaur by Theseus. There are records that just such a plaque was ripped up from the Chartres labyrinth during the Napoleonic era.

Craig Wright's 2001 academic book *The Maze and the Warrior* poses a whole new understanding of the medieval cathedral maze. Wright sees the defeat of the Minotaur by Theseus as symbolic of Christ's defeat of Satan in the harrowing of hell. There is only one rather obscure biblical reference to Christ's descent into hell and to his rescue of the souls trapped there. It appears in Ephesians 4:8–10 (RSV):

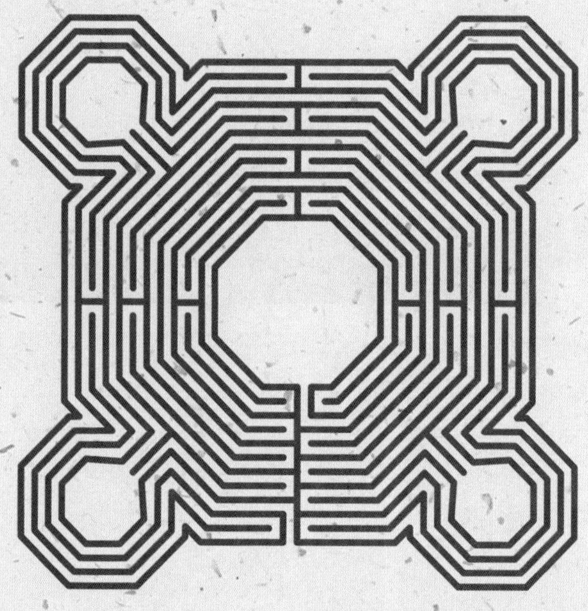

THE RHEIMS LABYRINTH

THE AMIENS LABYRINTH
(SAME PATTERN AS ST. QUENTIN)

> "When he ascended on high he led a host of captives, and he gave gifts to men." (In saying, "He ascended," what does it mean but that he had also descended into the lower parts of the earth? He who descended is he who also ascended far above all the heavens, that he might fill all things.)

Two hundred and fifty years after this was written it had solidified into the doctrine that, during his three days in the tomb, Jesus descended into hell, where he defeated Satan and preached to the souls of the dead, rescuing them from damnation. Wright argues convincingly that the medieval church identified Satan with the Minotaur and Christ

*Go to page 73 or 94*

with Theseus. Theseus' descent into the labyrinth prefigured Christ's descent into hell; Theseus' defeat of the Minotaur prefigured Christ's defeat of Satan. Wright presents evidence that, on Easter Monday, the cathedral clerics ritually reenacted Christ's defeat of Satan on the cathedral labyrinth, with much shouting. He has even produced medieval chants, which would have been used in the ritual to dance the labyrinth. In this view, Christ, like Theseus, is the warrior, the mythic hero, who defeats the forces of darkness, evil, and chaos, and who frees the captives once and for all.

From about 1500 CE onward, such monumental changes occurred that we talk about moving from the Medieval world to the modern world. Some historians write about moving from the age of faith to the age of reason. A few, specific examples illustrate the sorts of major, world-changing events that were happening in Europe. In 1492, Christopher Columbus landed in the New World, expanding Europeans' understanding of the extent and variety of other cultures, and sparking commerce. In 1517, Martin Luther nailed his 95 theses to the church door of Wittenberg, shattering the Christian consensus in Europe that had lasted more than 1000 years. In the 1540s, Gutenberg printed a German-language Bible, on the newly invented press with moveable type. This represented the beginning of the triumph of national languages over Latin as the language of learning. It was also the first glimpse of the technology which was to blossom over the next 500 years. The new Bible could also be mass produced and stirred a demand for people to learn to read. In 1543, Copernicus published his theory that the planets circled the sun, effectively refuting the official church position that the earth was the center of the universe and sowing the seed that would grow into modern science. In Italy, artists began to sign their work, prefiguring the rise of individualism; they also focused more often on secular subject matter. A new world was definitely coming into being.

The labyrinth was a victim of these changes. Protestant reformers (especially the radical Reformers, such as the Puritans) and the Roman Catholic counter-reformation disagreed on just about everything. But they *did* agree in their disparagement of anything with pagan roots. The labyrinth certainly had such roots, as the myth of Theseus and the Minotaur testifies.

In England, especially during the Commonwealth period of the 1650s when Puritans had supreme political power, the old turf labyrinths were abandoned and all forms of fertility celebrations were outlawed. Even when the monarchy was restored, these ancient practices never regained their former degree of energy. They became the passion of a few eccentrics, antiquarians, and rural folk. From time to time, some turf labyrinths were re-cut, but many were abandoned to revert to their natural state.

The cathedral labyrinths on the continent suffered a similar fate. Many clergy were suspicious of the pagan origins of the labyrinth; the practice of dancing in the church was also frowned upon. As

*Go to page 42, 44 or 75*

well, some clergy complained of being distracted by children playing in the labyrinth. As a result, many of the cathedral labyrinths were ripped up. Those that were not were covered over as an embarrassment to modern Christian sensibilities. Walking a simple path didn't seem to have much to do with religious faith in the complex new world that was emerging. The age of the labyrinth was coming to an end, though a fair number would be re-created, restored, or created during the Gothic revival of the 19th century.

## Experience

***The sound of the path 1:*** Some people find that they have their best experience of the labyrinth in complete silence. For many people, however, the use of appropriate music enhances their experience. You might try playing Medieval or early Renaissance music as you follow ancient and Medieval labyrinths. Gregorian chant would be a good choice. The archaic and slightly alien sound of the music to the modern sensibility matches well with ancient and slightly alien interpretations of the labyrinth.

***The interpretation of the path.*** You have encountered a great variety of labyrinths in this chapter and you have also encountered a great variety of interpretations. Maybe you have already experimented with putting labyrinth and interpretation together; if not, this experience gives you an opportunity to do so.

**1.** ***Death and resurrection, death and reincarnation, death and the afterlife.*** Ancient spirals at gravesites seem to have represented the descent into death and a coming back to whatever happens after death. You could try tracing the spiral on page 30 while contemplating death and new life. The path to the center could represent death, the path to the outside new life. Does this experience give you any new insights or any assurance?

**2.** ***The victory of reason over animal instinct.*** At a personal level, the seven-ringed Cretan labyrinth may be seen as representing the victory of our reason over our violent animal nature. Try tracing the labyrinth on page 10 while thinking about this. The path inward represents the descent into our violent and aggressive thoughts and instincts; at the center, our better human nature triumphs; as we move outward, our reason and benevolence lead us into the light of civilization. Was this a valuable exercise for you?

*Go to page 45 or 76*

3. ***The journey.*** Scandinavians walked rock labyrinths like the one on page 36 in preparation for a sea voyage. If you are going on a journey, you might try following this labyrinth as part of your preparations. Does this give you any sense of assurance?
4. For the North American Native hero, Siuku, the labyrinth was ***a path of safety and security,*** what today we call a safe place. As you trace various labyrinths, see what it feels like to imagine them as safe places in a dangerous world, safe paths through the unknown.
5. ***Thanksgiving.*** The English turf mazes were associated with fertility. You could use a labyrinth like the one at Saffron Walden (page 38) in thanksgiving for the regularity of the seasons. Suitable times for this are the solstices, the equinoxes, and full moons. You could also trace it as an act of gratitude for the bounty of the harvest on Thanksgiving.
6. ***Pilgrimage.*** We can't all go to Jerusalem or Mecca, or to bathe in the Ganges, but we *can* all go on pilgrimage in our imagination. Medieval cathedral labyrinths, like the ones on pages 40 and 42, were tools to help ordinary people who could not afford the pilgrimage. When you follow the sacred labyrinths presented in this chapter, is anything added to your understanding of pilgrimage? When you follow the different sacred paths, do you find that they lead to the same or different senses of pilgrimage?
7. ***Medieval cathedral labyrinths were sometimes called* daedale,** in remembrance of the first architect. As such, they recognized the creativity of the human spirit. They still can. Walking the labyrinth can be a way of focusing on and deriving inspiration for a creative project.
8. ***The harrowing of hell.*** In the Christian tradition, Jesus descended into hell to defeat Satan and to rescue the souls of those who were there. At the very least, this is a symbol of the defeat of evil, not so much the evil within us as the evil that comes from outside us. If you feel comfortable with this idea, try using your choice of cathedral labyrinths as a way of celebrating Christ's victory over evil. You might begin by reading a newspaper or watching a newscast; there will be enough evil and suffering there for your purposes. Then, trace the labyrinth, perhaps while singing one of the great triumphant hymns such as *Crown Him with Many Crowns* or *All Hail the Power of Jesus' Name.* Do you feel any sense of assurance that God is in charge?
9. ***Your personal meaning.*** If you have found that the labyrinth affects you spiritually in a particular way, try focusing on this as you experiment with the different types of labyrinths introduced in this chapter.

*Go to page 75 or 76*

Mirror Maze at Longleat, Wiltshire, UK

*Go to page 77 or 100*

# 3

# The Story of the Maze

## Experience

There are tricks you can use to help you solve mazes. The best known, in a full-sized maze, is to touch one of the walls with a hand, and to keep touching it with that hand as you walk through the maze, until you reach the center. With a paper maze, you can accomplish exactly the same effect by always taking the left path of two or more, or by always taking the right path. Like all of these tricks, this one won't work for all mazes, but it is always worth a try. Experiment with this on the Hampton Court maze on page 11. First, try always taking the left-hand path. Then, try always taking the right-hand path. Now try the same thing with the maze to the right.

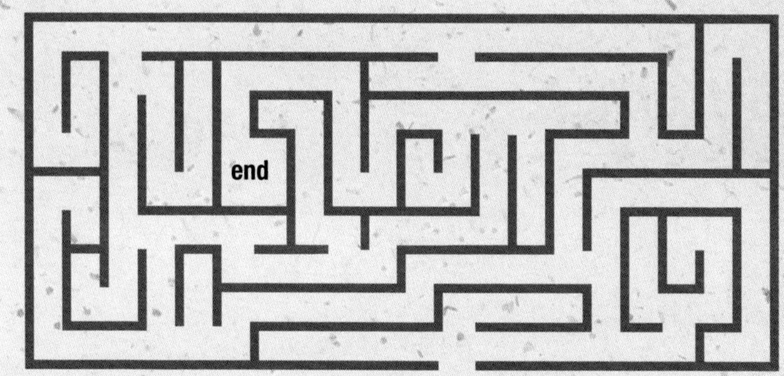


Why do you suppose that it didn't work this time? Remember that the whole purpose of a maze is to fool you.

*Go to page 12 or 100*

Another trick is to start at the end and find your way to the entrance. Try that with the maze on page 11 and the one on page 47.

Do you feel as if you are cheating somehow?

Why or why not?

What would happen when you're not sure where the entrance is, or which path leads from the end toward it? Of course, this technique will not work with hedge mazes or other mazes where the end is not visible.

It is not just solving a maze that is important; it is solving it elegantly, finding the shortest path from the entrance to the end. This can be done easily and accurately for many mazes using the following method. Just follow the path always turning to the left. Whenever you encounter a dead end and have to retrace your path, mark the part retraced with a pencil or marker. Finish solving the maze using only left-hand turnings and marking all retraced paths. Now do it again using only right-hand turnings and marking retraced paths. The first step, to the right, illustrates how to mark the first dead end for the Hampton Court maze; the second step illustrates all the passages that will be filled in when you reach the center by choosing only left-hand turnings; the third step shows all the passages that will he filled in when you have solved the maze by adding right-hand turnings. The part of the path that is left clear is the elegant solution, the shortest route from entrance to end.

Psychologists tell us that rats discover the shortest path in a maze by trial and error, by trying every path and dismissing those that don't work,

just as you have done. Then, they run the maze accurately after that. Try doing the Hampton Court maze (page 11) as quickly as you can, to see if this maze learning technique has worked for you.

Finally, when solving two-dimensional mazes such as these, you can always try to look ahead in order to avoid dead ends. This is generally an effective technique, but as mazes become more complex it becomes less useful.

*Go to page 79 or 100*

## To Begin With

Mazes were created as diversions, for fun. There is something satisfying about finding your way despite all the obstacles that stand in your path, despite false starts and twists and turns and dead ends. In the end, solving the maze is about personal accomplishment. Perhaps the need to find one's own way in the maze stems from the same impulse that makes men, according to common wisdom anyway, unwilling to ask for directions. Yet, although it may feel like a solitary enterprise, the maze is actually the ground for a battle of wits, which pits the ingenuity of the maze designer against the cleverness or, sometimes, the sheer persistence of the maze walker.

## The Garden Maze

One of the most obvious characteristic of garden mazes is their transience. They are, after all, part of a garden, usually made from some sort of vegetation. They can be dug up to plant a bed of roses. If they are ignored, they quickly overgrow or die off. They are subject to natural processes and require constant attention. So we do not usually have very old garden mazes. The wonder is that we have a few that date back to the 17th century, such as the Hampton Court maze.

What we do have from a century earlier are plans for garden mazes. Here is a design for a topiary garden maze intended for Charleval, a town in Normandy. The maze was designed by Androuet du Cerceau (1520–1584), for the palace gardens. Though the gardens still exist, and are on European garden tours, there is no trace of the palace and we do not know whether the maze was ever planted.

Maze at Charleval

*Go to page 50 or 78*

The materials out of which garden mazes were made varied. Some early mazes were made of turf, like the English turf labyrinths. Others, such as the knot gardens, were made in aromatic herb beds. Both of these types of mazes were relatively easy to solve; you could just look ahead and avoid dead ends. Eventually, hedges became more or less standard, using relatively dense and closely grown shrubs or trees such as cedar, box, or yew. Sometimes, the branches of limes or hornbeams would be trained to interweave to create a dense wall.

The direct antecedents of the garden maze are uncertain. Early garden turf mazes suggest that the much larger English turf mazes, actually labyrinths, may have been their model. Herb knot gardens were popular because they allowed easy access to the herbs and were very attractive. They also might have been the model for the first garden mazes. However, neither the turf labyrinth nor the knot garden contained a puzzle; this was the contribution of the landscape architects of the 16th and 17th centuries who designed the first garden mazes for which we have drawings.

A KNOT GARDEN

Landscape architects introduced complications. The beautiful 19th-century maze at Hatfield House, which still exists, has two entrances.

THE HATFIELD HOUSE MAZE

The maze at Versailles (see page 51) introduced a different type of puzzle. To solve this maze, enter at the lower right-hand corner and visit every statue (marked in dark green) without crossing your path or without retracing any part of your path unless you reach a dead end, which actually does happen once in the correct solution. The actual layout of the paths at Versailles does not constitute a maze, but the puzzle instructions turn it into one.

*Go to page 79 or 100*

The Versailles Maze

*Go to page 14 or 50*

# MAKING IT HARDER

By the 19th century, the standard garden maze was no challenge. Everyone had heard about placing one hand on a wall and just walking until the center was reached. It was not a very elegant solution, but it was an effective and guaranteed solution. So maze designers introduced a number of geometrical and/or psychological features to trick the mind and fool the eye.

It is significant that mazes became more difficult as the problems of life became more complex, with increasing industrialization and the urbanization of Europe, and with the complex bureaucracies associated with the spread of European empires abroad.

The credit for devising a maze that cannot be solved by placing one hand on a wall and walking is generally given to the 2nd Earl of Stanhope, who was a mathematician as well as an aristocrat. His hedge maze at Chevening House is, in effect, two independent mazes one embedded within the other. This ingenious feature means that using the method of always keeping either your right or left hand on the wall will just bring you back to the entrance. The maze solver has to change tactics and it is difficult to see just what tactic will be effective. Unfortunately, this maze is not open to the public for reasons of national security. It is not that the maze is a state secret, but that the current occupant of Chevening House is the British Foreign Secretary.

I have known for a long time about some of the psychological tricks that maze designers use to fool us. However, it is difficult to spot them in a two-dimensional maze. So it was delightful to experience some of them firsthand at Chatsworth. Once you pay your fee to enter the vast grounds of Chatsworth, the home of the Duke of Devonshire, the maze is free. It is set in vast, magnificently landscaped grounds. It had rained recently and I had to jump a few puddles on the paths. But it wasn't the puddles that caused my confusion. I have to give the maze designer credit for fooling me not once but

THE CHEVENING HOUSE HEDGE MAZE

*Go to page 53 or 81*

several times. On paper, the Chatsworth maze looks very easy. However, the real hedge maze, while not large, is tricky. The maze is square with a circular maze within it. As you enter, you may go to the left or right on a straight path forming a square all the way around the circular maze. Most right-handed people will turn right without even thinking; I am right-handed. I knew better, but I fell for it anyway. Had I turned left, the next right turn leads relatively directly to the center.

I will describe my progress through the maze as it would appear on the two-dimensional copy to the right, though, of course, the real maze doesn't have a top or a bottom. Coming into the circle from the top, I naturally turned right and found several dead ends and no path forward. When I got back to the upper opening and looked down the path ahead, it looked exactly like the dead ends behind me so I went back out onto the straight path, turning right again. At the bottom, I went back into the circle and had the opportunity to explore two more corners full of dead ends. Back at the top, I entered the circle and glanced to my left, still a dead end. So I turned right. I just wasn't all that sure that I had explored this section. Of course, I didn't find anything new. Finally, I decided to walk all the way to the dead end in the upper right corner of the maze, only what I found was not a dead end but a path to my left going right into the corner, then coming back into the circular maze. Another trick in this maze is having paths that seem to lead away from the center being the correct path, while paths that seem to lead to the center are just dead ends. Finally, there are places where it is obvious that you should go forward on your path when, actually, you must take the less-obvious opening that appears to be just another diversion. This beautiful maze is relatively modern, but it is based on a design from old papers found in Chatsworth House. I know of no example of a hedge maze that illustrates the maze designer's tricks so well. Or was I just particularly muddled as well as muddied that day at Chatsworth?

The Chatsworth House Maze

*Go to page 16 or 82*

# THE MAZE THAT BEHAVES LIKE A LABYRINTH

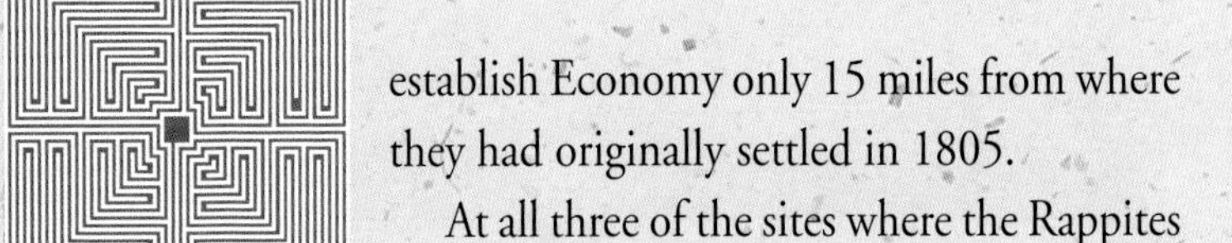

In the early 1800s, utopian communities sprang up all over the Western world. Often, in Europe, such communities ran into hostility, either from the government or from neighbors. One such community was the Rappites, founded by George Rapp in Germany. In 1803 Rapp, with a collection of followers, migrated to the United States and settled in Pennsylvania, where, by 1805, they set up their own community called Harmony. Ten years later they moved to Indiana, where they established New Harmony. They felt that both the land and the neighbors there were inhospitable, so in 1824 they sold New Harmony to Robert Owen for his own experiment in communal living. The Rappites moved back to Pennsylvania to establish Economy only 15 miles from where they had originally settled in 1805.

At all three of the sites where the Rappites tried to establish communities, they built vine mazes or perhaps vine labyrinths. It seems more likely that they were mazes since they were intended to symbolize the difficulty of establishing a harmonious community. In other words, these mazes have religious symbolism. Unlike most other mazes, they are not just diversions; they are more like a sacrament, a visible sign of the Rappites' inner faith. Sometimes, it seems that even mazes can surprise us by functioning as though they are labyrinths, representing the truths of specific religious beliefs.

NEW HARMONY MAZE, INDIANA

THE 1939 NEW HARMONY MAZE

*Go to page 18 or 19*

The symbolism went beyond the maze at New Harmony to include a little temple at the center. This building was constructed of rough wood. Inside, the building was beautifully finished. The exterior of the building represented the world with all its difficulties; the interior symbolized the perfection of the ideal community, for which the Rappites strove.

By the mid 19th century, all three of these mazes had fallen into such disrepair that even the outlines of the maze could no longer be discerned. In 1939, as part of a restoration project, a new hedge maze was planted at New Harmony in keeping with the intent of the designers of the original maze, though not to the original design which had been lost. This maze has three entrances and there are three paths from the center. Any wrong choice can lead to a dead end, a loop, or even back out onto the lawn behind the maze.

So it is possible for a maze to be intended to have a spiritual meaning. The Rappites' faith was not about submitting to God's given path, as symbolized by the labyrinth; it was about striving to carve out their own community against all odds. The maze was a far more fitting symbol of the Rappites' hopes and dreams and faith – a faith well-fitted to its time.

## CHILD'S PLAY

By the early 20th century, garden mazes had gone out of fashion. We are fortunate that some mazes were preserved and that a number more have been restored in the last 30 years. The reasons that mazes went out of fashion are not clear. Perhaps the intensely practical mindset of the wealthy landowners, who were by and large industrialists, saw mazes as a waste of time and space, both of which could be better used to generate income. Perhaps the drastic reduction of holy days, accompanied by a significant increase in hours of work for most people, didn't leave time for such frivolities as mazes. Perhaps the seriousness of life and religion in Victorian times was not symbolized well by the playfulness of the maze. Perhaps people had become tired of mazes and were looking for something new. Perhaps the cost of upkeep was too great. Whatever the reasons, interest in garden mazes gradually diminished during the early 20th century.

For some reason, when an adult fashion ends it is often passed on to children. Children's clothing often reflects adult styles from a generation or two before. Nineteenth-century adult social protest novels, such as *Black Beauty* and *Uncle Tom's Cabin,* came to be seen in the 20th century as children's

*Go to page 17 or 20*

literature. Of course, it is not universally true that adult fashions are passed on to children of a later generation, but it *does* happen.

Something like this happened to the maze. By the end of the 19th century, children's maze toys appeared on the market. The first and most enduring of these was called "Pigs in Clover." This was a pocket-sized, sealed, circular maze containing a number of ball bearings. The object of the puzzle was to manipulate all the bearings through the maze to the goal at the center. Usually, this was done by tilting the puzzle, but some had convex bases that would not allow for tilting. In these toys, the bearings had to be manipulated with a magnet. Most Pigs in Clover were real mazes, but some simply contained concentric circles with breaks, without dead ends or switchbacks. These puzzles could be slipped into a pocket and carried anywhere. Over time, more and more ingenious maze games were designed for children, including different shaped mazes and even three-dimensional mazes. For a short period of time, the ball bearings were even replaced by a drop of mercury. We can think of these maze games as low-tech precursors to the electronic games of the late 20th century. I suspect that parents, then, as now, had to tell their children to put their games away and get on with their homework.

Another late Victorian use of mazes appeared in traveling carnivals, which sometimes featured a mirror maze. Mirror mazes had the advantage of being portable and easily erected and dismantled. Most of them included both clear glass and mirrored walls, which compounded the confusion. Often, the center of the maze, or alternatively the entrance, contained distorting mirrors in which walkers could see themselves with short legs, or huge heads, or practically no heads at all. It was all wonderful fun, especially for children who constituted the majority of mirror maze walkers. The mirror maze was one of the delights of my own childhood, right up there with cotton candy, whenever the carnival came to town.

TWO VERSIONS OF PIGS IN CLOVER

*Go to page 21 or 22*

## WHAT WAS IT ALL ABOUT?

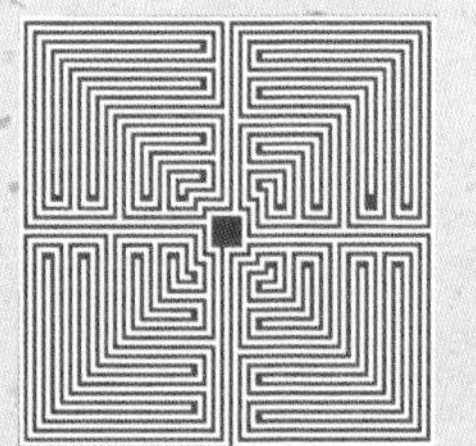

The shift in popularity from the sacred labyrinth to the secular maze, during the 16th century, seems to me to have been a barometer signaling a radical shift in spirituality. It is not that people became less religious. Rather, the nature of their religion changed. Medieval religion was largely experiential. Because most people could not read, their ideas about God were mediated by the spectacle of the mass, by the multitude of holy days and the rituals associated with them, and by the wonder of the Gothic churches. Education, the printing press, and the Protestant Reformation brought a new kind of religion – one focused on the mind rather than on the senses. God was now mediated by the Bible and by the sermon. The Word was to be experienced through words. The radical reformers, in particular, made a conscious and deliberate attempt to reduce sensory input so that the mind could focus on ideas. As part of this program, they simplified church buildings, and severely restricted the use of adornments and artwork of all kinds. Some traditions even banned the use of musical instruments. Though these things happened in relatively smaller and in some instances fringe groups, their influence was important. For example, Isaac Newton, the father of physics, was a lifelong member of just such a group. It was, at least partly, his faith that led him to believe that the world must be orderly and understandable.

A second aspect of this shift in spirituality was the separation of the sacred and the secular. From the Renaissance and Reformation on, a growing erosion of the role of religion in fields like art and commerce developed. Artists began to paint and sculpt purely secular objects and to sign their works forgoing the pretense that art was done for the glory of God; art was done for its own sake.

During the Medieval age, the church had held doctrines about the appropriate way in which business was to be conducted. Boys were expected to take up their father's profession. Ambition was the sin that caused Satan to be cast from heaven. Prices should not go up, because God instituted the value of all things once and for all time. The fact that none of these doctrines were actually applied universally, and at times were not applied at all, does not mean that people did not believe them.

As the new era unfolded, the opening of colonies all over the world created huge business opportunities. Pilgrimages and crusades gave way to commerce and the spirit of adventure as reasons for travel. The Medieval system of commerce was turned on its head. What had been virtues became vices, and vice versa. Boys were expected to do whatever work would bring the most money. Ambition became a virtue, in fact, *the* virtue, as far as business and commerce were concerned. The fair price was the highest price you could get away with. There was

*Go to page 59 or 85*

a new spirit in the air – a secular spirit, so to speak.

It is not likely that people consciously chose the puzzle maze as a symbol of the new spirit of the times; such choices are more unconscious than deliberate. Yet the maze was an ideal symbol to represent the new spirit of science and secularity, because it represented individual decision, responsibility, reason, and competition. It was a symbol of private wealth rather than public devotion. It was secular and rational. As one element of the garden of a wealthy estate, it represented the power of people to tame nature, to shape it into something better, something more beautiful, more useful, more essentially human. The maze reflected the spirit of the times almost perfectly.

## Experience

***The sound of the path 2:***

The maze developed in the context of what we call classical music and so, if you enjoy having music playing while doing mazes, almost any secular classical music would be an appropriate accompaniment. The complexity of a Bach fugue would be suitable with a complex maze. But most secular music should make a pleasant background for maze solving.

Mazes are puzzles. They are designed to challenge you. Many people like this sort of challenge; they get a sense of satisfaction from solving puzzles, or from solving them faster than other people, or from finding the most elegant solution. What, if anything, gives you satisfaction in solving mazes? Go back and redo the mazes in this book focusing on your particular source of satisfaction. What, if anything, have you learned about yourself? About the way you relate to challenge in everyday life? About the way you relate to other people? About the way you relate to the world?

Designing mazes can be as much fun as solving them. We can create mazes of varying complexity and give them to friends to enjoy. Here are a few tips for designing mazes; all of the original mazes in this book were designed in this way.

Start with the correct solution. On a piece of graph paper, lay out the shape of the maze and the

*Go to page 86 or 87*

location of its entrance and end. (I used graph paper to create the maze below, but you can draw freeform mazes with curving paths just as well.) Next, draw your planned shortest path between them as in the diagram below.

***First step in designing a maze***

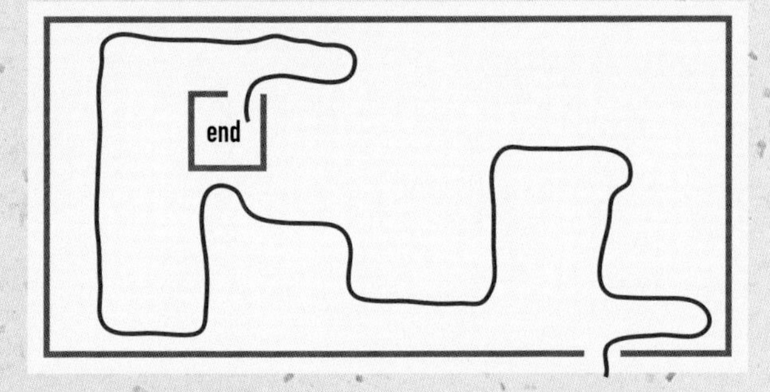


Now add lots of dead ends and loops, as in the second step, below. Put in the walls, as in the third step. Finally, trace only the walls to form a standard maze pattern, as in the fourth step. The result is a maze of the early sort that can be solved by placing a hand on either wall and walking to the center.

***Second step in designing a maze***

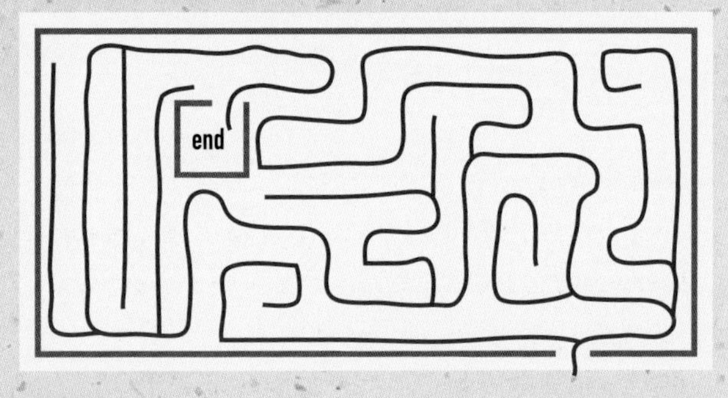


***Third step in designing a maze***

***Fourth step in designing a maze***

If you would like a more complex maze pattern, one which cannot be solved by placing one hand on a wall and walking, all you need to do is make sure that there is a central path that completely surrounds the goal, as indicated by the dotted line in the diagram on the next page. Then, follow the second, third, and fourth steps above to create a maze something like the one page 61.

If you are interested in creating a really complex maze like the Chevening hedge maze, the pattern for it is given on the following page. The two patterns actually overlap. The loop coming from the entrance is marked with dashes; the one coming from the center is marked with dots. Note how they overlap, but, if you check them out, they run in opposite directions. This sort of integration is very difficult to accomplish, but very satisfying and quite difficult to solve, especially in an actual hedge maze.

*Go to page 23 or 26*

The Chevening Hedge Maze Analyzed

*Go to page 27 or 28*

# 4

# A Journey into Symbolism

## EXPERIENCE

This chapter documents my own growing discovery of labyrinths and mazes as spiritual symbols, and their increasing meaning in my life. The experience that follows is a good place to explore *your own* relationship to spiritual symbols, whatever they may be.

The symbol that I am suggesting you explore is the traditional Christian symbol of the cross and/or crucifix. If you are not comfortable using this symbol, you can use the same exercise for any other spiritual symbol or symbolic action, such as the yin-yang symbol in Taoism; the *ohm* sound in Buddhism; fasting in Islam; the four directions in Native North American spirituality; earth, air, fire, and water in ancient Greek philosophy; or any symbol of your choice. The symbol should be one, though, that has had growing meaning for you.

What makes religious and spiritual symbols so powerful is the fact that we can never fully comprehend them. Just when we think we understand their ultimate meaning another layer peels away and we see hidden depths. They are never through with us. If we fix the meaning of symbols, we cease to be open to new truth. This is a form of idolatry, substituting our ideas for the Ultimate. So, in this exercise, we should not expect final answers; only God is final. Rather, we should expect to meet ourselves. We are creating spiritual biography, not theology.

Try to find as many symbolic meanings for the cross (or your chosen alternative) as you can, even those which you do not find personally meaningful, even those with which you may disagree. For example, at different times and in different places the cross has held one or more of these meanings for various people:

*Go to page 28 or 62*

- a humiliating form of capital punishment for criminal slaves and foreigners
- the intersection of earth (the horizontal) and heaven (the vertical)
- a relic having miraculous powers
- human sin and folly
- the sacrifice of God's child
- a blood offering for sin
- God's self-offering
- judgment
- forgiveness

There are many other symbolic ways of understanding the cross. Please add others that you think of to this list.

Now think about the first time you can remember being aware of the cross. What was that experience like? What did it mean to you then? How did your understanding of the cross grow and change later? What experiences went into these changes? What is your most recent experience of the cross? What does it mean to you now?

## TO BEGIN WITH

Your spiritual journey has been extremely complex. Everyone's has. You have had many experiences, grown through many crises, celebrated many victories, found meaning in many symbols. This is true of me, too. So the little slice of spiritual biography in this chapter is just that: a little slice. It is the story of my adventures with mazes and labyrinths and that is all that it is. This chapter deals with only these two symbols.

This limitation is the reason that I hope that my story might be helpful to you. Since this is a book about labyrinths and mazes, it seems obvious that my journey with these symbols may help you to think about your own. Beyond this, I also hope that this chapter may help you to think about the role of other symbols in your spiritual journey.

*Go to page 62 or 63*

## Childhood Mazes

I do not know where or how I first encountered mazes – I suspect that it may have been in Sunday school papers – but my first *memory* of them is from comic books. I loved comic books, collected them, and traded them, despite my mother's fear that the comic books I got from other children would harbor bedbugs. I kept them in a cardboard box under my bed and hauled them out on rainy afternoons, spreading them lovingly about the floor to organize and reorganize them. One feature of many of these comics was a puzzle page with a rebus, a crossword, a conundrum, and, best of all, a maze. These mazes contained a story about the comic heroes: Mighty Mouse rescuing Pauline from Oil Can Harry, Captain Marvel defeating the forces of evil. I don't remember exactly what I thought about them, but I do know that I was, even then, able to separate the story from the maze, because I did exactly that.

I drew vast mazes on the floor of our basement with colored chalk and invited my friends over for a maze party. Already, at probably ten or 11 years of age, I recognized the integrity of the maze apart from the story imposed on it in the comic books. When I try to think about my motivation for these maze parties, I suspect that I really just wanted to fool my friends.

But I also created mazes just for my own pleasure. On wet days and long winter evenings, I lay on the living room rug constructing ever more complex mazes out of toothpicks. My electric train and bicycle never gave me the hours of fun that I could get from a box of toothpicks and the mazes that swarmed through my imagination.

My friend Don was one of the most competitive people I have ever known. We learned chess from the encyclopedia, and, with many arguments about rules, Don beat me consistently. I remember him visiting me when I was sick in bed and we spent an afternoon creating mazes for each other. I felt that his weren't fair. Paths narrowed or widened at his whim; sometimes it was impossible to tell whether

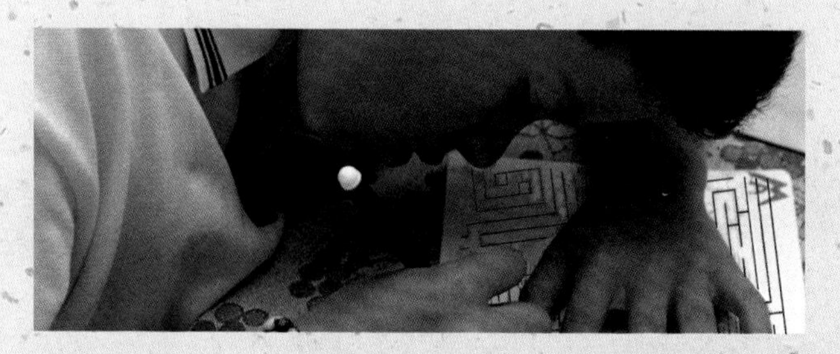

a gap was a real pathway or just bad drawing. The mazes in comic books were never like that. I realize now that he was using tricks that real maze designers commonly use, but in childhood it seemed that he wasn't playing fair. I didn't say anything. I didn't want to do anything that would prevent me from designing my own mazes to try to fool him.

*Go to page 30 or 91*

## GROWN-UP MAZES

As I grew up, I had to satisfy my maze cravings with occasional maze magazines and mirror mazes at carnivals. Maze magazines were published, but rarely, by the same people who published crosswords and word searches. They usually involved a time challenge and the drawing was pretty standard, bigger than comic book mazes and without a story, but using the same principles. Mirror mazes were more dramatic because they were full-sized, using both clear glass and mirrors to confuse the solver. You could actually walk through them. They were something pretty special at the time.

Then I discovered W. H. Matthews' book *Mazes and Labyrinths: Their History and Development.* This book, first published in 1922 and still in print, remains a seminal treatment, though there have been many recent developments and discoveries. With over 150 photographs, line drawings, and facsimiles from old manuscripts, a whole new world of mazes and labyrinths opened for me. Now I was interested not just to fool my friends; labyrinths and mazes had become objects of beauty and elegance and their history and origins were shrouded in mystery.

I was hooked on both labyrinths and mazes. Over the years, I began to collect maze books. At first, these books were pretty standard, but they gradually became more elaborate and eccentric and very large. The mazes themselves added new dimensions and became increasingly complex. They incorporated bridges and tunnels, words and numbers, puzzles within puzzles, until, at least for me, they were no longer solvable puzzles, but objects to be collected for their curiosity. They came to represent for me the ever increasing complexity of life, which often involves elements of which we are not even aware.

I also encountered the occasional full-sized maze. The most memorable was the hedge maze planted on Centre Island, Toronto, in 1967, to celebrate Canada's centennial. At the time I walked it, the hedges had just been planted, but it would have become a challenging walk over the years. It has been replaced with a grass maze of the same pattern, not exactly the challenge it could have been.

One other interesting maze encounter was in the film *The Shining.* The hero/villain of Stephen

*Go to page 32 or 67*

A Maize Maze

King's novel was killed by topiary figures; in the film, he froze to death, lost in a hedge maze. This was the first time it occurred to me that my beloved mazes might be seen as horrific objects. Perhaps this is one reason that I didn't like the film at first, though it has grown on me over time. As an aside, the maze used in the film was the Tree Tops Maze, at Carleton near Yarmouth, Nova Scotia. In 1995, it was reported to be in poor shape and was closed to the public.

At the same time that I was encountering all these mazes, I found myself becoming more moved by the labyrinth, especially after I saw some of the ancient labyrinth sites for myself. A picture of a labyrinth is beautiful, but seeing the original is a moving, spiritually transformative experience.

Hedge Maze, Leeds Castle, UK

*Go to page 32, 33 or 92*

ONE OF THE ROCKY VALLEY LABYRINTHS

*Go to page 67 or 92*

## ROCKY VALLEY

During May and June of 1986, Joyce and I walked a good part of the South West Coast Path in England. This trail runs for 520 miles, from Minehead in Somerset, to Poole in Dorset. Most of the trail runs within sight of the sea. It was a splendid, strenuous, spiritual adventure; a pilgrimage into ancient times, in the constant presence of the ever-changing, equally ancient sea.

In north Cornwall, there is a little combe, a valley cut down to the ocean by a stream. Rocky Valley, as it is called, lies halfway between Tintagel and Boscastle.

Legend has it that, one dark night, King Arthur was conceived at Tintagel, through deception and magic. The town has become terribly commercialized with the Camelot Café and the King Arthur Service Station. Yet some magic still clings to the ancient ruined monastery, and even more to St. Materiana's Church, on the cliff overlooking the town. St. Materiana's parish was founded, like many parishes along the north Cornish coast, by Irish missionaries, most of them said to be excess, unmarried Celtic princesses.

Tintagel sits two miles west of Rocky Valley. Two miles east of Rocky Valley is Boscastle, which was, for many centuries, reputed to be a major center for Cornish witchcraft, and which now has a very interesting museum devoted to witches and witchcraft. Cornish witchcraft is said to be concerned primarily with healing, and with securing fair winds for sailors and fishers who navigated this extremely dangerous coast.

Halfway between Tintagel and Boscastle, as I said, lies the combe called Rocky Valley. I was alone the first time I saw it and I was entranced. Where the stream runs into the ocean there is a tiny reversing falls. When the tide is out, fresh water from the stream tumbles into the ocean; when the tide is in, salt water spills over a rock ridge to fall into the stream. When I first saw it, it seemed to defy nature, with the ocean falling into the stream. Walking upstream, I was surrounded by massed bluebells and wild garlic that smelled like French cooking. Eventually, I came to a waterfall, with a tearoom at the top. The story goes that, in the second century, a Christian hermit came from somewhere in the Mediterranean and established a hermitage, where the tearoom sits today. This was St. Nectan; the waterfall is known as St. Nectan's Cleve. It falls through a large hole in the rock and seems to twist in midair as it does so. At the base of the falls is a huge flat rock under which are buried, according to tradition, St. Nectan's two sisters, who were feared as witches by local people.

Halfway between the ocean and the waterfall is a ruined mill and on the rock cliff face behind it are two carved labyrinths, each about 7.25" (18 cm) in diameter. A metal plaque dates these carvings

*Go to page 36 or 94*

between 1800 and 1400 BCE, but antiquarians disagree among themselves about their actual age. Some believe them to be of ancient origin, carved, perhaps, by Phoenician sailors who are reported to have come as far as Cornwall to pick up precious tin; others believe that they are of Christian origin and date them much later; a few scholars even try to date them from the time of the industrial revolution, when a mill was built on the site. Local legend, as told through the person of the tearoom lady, says that one of the labyrinths is ancient and one is a relatively modern copy, but no one knows which is which.

Wildflower Offering Placed at a Rocky Valley Labyrinth

My own sense of these labyrinths is that they are truly ancient and that, even if they are not, they convey ancient wisdom. I do not know what they were intended to symbolize in a literal sense, in the sense of "this" object standing for "that" truth. Whether they represented the womb, or the journey to the underworld and back in reincarnation, or pilgrimage, really didn't matter to me at that moment. I only knew that I was in the presence of something old, and archetypal, and mysterious – something magic.

It wasn't just the labyrinth carvings. There was magic in the waterfall and in the stream and in the bluebells, and in the ruins of the mill. Magic hung in the warm spring air. Yet I can't help believing that all of that magic emanated *from* the carvings. I was in a sacred space.

I followed the labyrinth paths, first one, then the other, with my eyes – one does not touch sacred objects without permission. I knew then, as I have known ever since, that this was what I had been searching for. It was not that mazes ceased to be fun and frustrating and powerful symbols of the modern condition, for me. It was just that in these labyrinths, in the wild, I met something universal and profound and sacred, something mysterious that I could never fully understand.

When I returned the next day, it was still beautiful, but the air was no longer suffused with magic. We can't expect wonder to come at our command; it is a mystery and a gift. The stream was just a charming stream, the bluebells just beautiful flowers. Only

*Go to page 36, 94 or 110*

the labyrinths remained sacred and mysterious. And even now, still, I experience that sense of being on sacred ground, whenever I think about them.

Many Internet sites feature these carvings. More recent pilgrims have found the site changed by those who have left offerings – strips of cloth tied to tree branches, flowers in crevasses – and even more changed by those who try to spoil what they cannot understand, with graffiti and litter. Yet despite offerings and litter and graffiti, pilgrims still write about the magic they have felt in that place. I was lucky. The site was unspoiled when I was there. There was nothing to stand between me and the magic.

## Saffron Walden

The attendant at the Saffron Walden Tourist Office told us to follow the footpath leading from the parking lot across the common. But there was no footpath and the famous turf labyrinth was nowhere in sight. The common itself may once have been a field for grazing sheep on the edge of town; today it is surrounded by streets with houses and parked cars. Across the common we could see a low mound covered with grass, so we set out for that.

I don't know what I was expecting – perhaps something like the white horse of Uffington or the Cerne Abbas Giant, something obviously dramatic. After all, this is the largest turf labyrinth on public land in England, and, like those chalk figures, it is probably a symbol of fertility. Its origins are lost in mystery; its purpose only half understood. I was expecting to be knocked off my feet.

But at first glance, the labyrinth was underwhelming. It was much smaller than I expected; smaller, for example, than the stone and grass labyrinth at a convent in North Bay, Ontario, a little more than an hour's drive from my home. I had come all the way to England for this? It was surrounded by a low earthwork called a berm, which effectively hid it from view until we were almost upon it.

*Go to page 37 or 94*

The labyrinth itself is a narrow track cut in the turf. In recent times, bricks have been laid in the track to make upkeep easier. Less than a foot of grass separates the tracks, which is why the whole thing fits into such a compact area. There is a large open mound in the center and four petal-like forms coming out from the circular labyrinth. (See photograph below and illustration on page 38.)

My first inkling that things were not as simple as they seemed came when I tried to photograph the labyrinth. There was no way to get a picture of the whole thing. When I stood on the berm, I could only get a portion of the labyrinth in the frame; if I backed down off the berm, a good part of my view was blocked. I realized that it would be just as difficult to draw it. Unlike most labyrinths, the one at Saffron Walden is truly a three-dimensional object. The mounds in which the petals are embedded, and especially the large central mound, are as essential to this labyrinth as the path itself.

Then I began to walk the labyrinth. The narrow path, the width of a single brick, demanded my complete attention. Gradually, my sense of the present fell away. I completely forgot about cars and houses and the town that surrounded me; by the time I had walked two or three rings, it was the *labyrinth* that surrounded me with a sense of something ancient and mysterious and unbelievably calm. And the path *was* long, far longer than any other labyrinth I had walked. This was the effect of packing so much path into such a small space. The petal shapes, each with three paths running through it, come almost at the end of the path, as though to say "You have to go far away from the center, back out into the world, before you can reach your goal." Surprisingly, I did not sense fertility, either on the path or at its center, but rather peace and power. The whole experience was very different than any other experience I have had of the labyrinth.

*Go to page 40 or 95*

## CHARTRES

It is only a small step from the turf labyrinth to the Christian cathedral labyrinth – not a literal step from one geometric pattern to another so much as a step from one religious mindset to another. Gradually, the idea came to me that something important had happened around 1500. The labyrinth was discarded and mazes were born; an old worldview was cast aside and the modern world came into being. There must have been some connection, I reasoned, if only a symbolic one. Because no one seemed to have noticed the connection, I decided to write an academic article about this. Or maybe subconsciously all I really wanted was an excuse to visit mazes and labyrinths. Whatever was in my mind, in 1989 I found myself walking the most famous labyrinth in the world, at Chartres Cathedral. (See the illustration on page 40.)

Actually, walking may not be the best word to describe my progress into the heart of this labyrinth. There were chairs over part of the labyrinth and some of the time I was creeping over and around them. But even chairs could not spoil the wonder of this largest and most detailed of cathedral labyrinths, which was built into the stone floor, in the nave, directly under the west, or main, entrance. The rose window gives the impression of being the same size as the labyrinth and the same height above the floor that the labyrinth is distant from the doors. Though the optics of stained glass make it impossible, I could not help feeling that, on just the right day of the year, at just the right time of the evening, the light of the rose window would fall directly upon the labyrinth, covering it precisely; very much like the rising sun of the winter solstice pierces the burial mounds at Newgrange.

Recent findings suggest that sacred geometry – ancient secret knowledge about the effect of shape and forms upon the human spirit – permeates Chartres cathedral and its labyrinth. Certainly, the experience of walking any labyrinth, and especially this one, is far more powerful than just another walk. I knew this long before I knew anything about sacred geometry, of course, but I am sure that unconsciously the geometry touched me at Chartres, as it has touched so many others.

that occurred within her as she walked the labyrinth. As we follow her, we move through hell and heaven, guilt and expiation, despair and hope. In the end, she carried all this out of the cathedral and into the world, the true labyrinth of which the labyrinth in Chartres cathedral is but a model. In Travers, all of this is informed by the sensibility of a self-proclaimed skeptical seeker. It is hard to imagine two more different pilgrims to Chartres, yet each in her own way found transformative power in the labyrinth.

Lauren Artress and P. L. Travers have testified to the labyrinth's psychological and spiritual power in very different ways and from very different perspectives. Dr. Artress is Canon for Special Ministries at Grace Cathedral in San Francisco. She is also the primary driving force in the recent revival of labyrinth spirituality, which will be discussed in the last chapter. In her book *Walking a Sacred Path,* she described very little of her actual experience of walking the Chartres labyrinth, but she was so deeply affected that she wrote in retrospect that she "had received the embrace of Mary." On the other hand, in her book *What the Bee Knows,* Travers, who is best known as the creator of *Mary Poppins,* gave us a detailed, almost step-by-step account of the psychological and spiritual changes

As I walked the labyrinth at Chartres, I sensed that I was retracing my own spiritual journey, from early childhood fundamentalism, through what I think of as superstitious agnosticism, to liberal Christianity, then through doubt and despair to glimmerings of hope and beyond. Putting it another way, I walked through my grandmother's religion, my friends' religion, my father's religion, and my own religion – and then began moving into something else, something new. The Chartres labyrinth was, for me, the path of hope.

Yet for all that hope, the Chartres labyrinth carries in itself reminders of the arrogance, superstition, and fear that have always been present in human

*Go to page 43 or 44*

history and in me. It is hard for me to imagine the small-mindedness of the bureaucracy that ripped the ancient copper plaque from the center of the labyrinth to make ammunition for Napoleon's army. It is even harder to imagine the fear of the church bureaucracy that covered up or destroyed cathedral labyrinths all over southern Europe. It was not because they did not recognize the spiritual power of the labyrinth; it was because they *did* recognize it and they feared it.

I suspect that the rebirth of the Chartres labyrinth had already begun by the time I walked it. In 1984, five years earlier, the cathedral published an edition of their magazine *Notre-dame du Chartres,* devoted to their own and other cathedral labyrinths. Today the labyrinth in Chartres cathedral is walked, and even danced, by visiting clergy arranged by the cathedral. We can only celebrate the spiritual enlightenment that caused this change in church policy and the spiritual enlightenment that this change in policy will bring to the hearts of worshippers.

Yet I am glad that I experienced the labyrinth through a maze of chairs, because this so fittingly symbolized the barriers to spiritual fulfillment that existed in European history and in my own life; it so perfectly symbolized our spiritual journey as a people over the last 500 years, and my own spiritual journey over the last almost 60, as we, and I, stumbled toward enlightenment.

## Crete

When Joyce and I flew to Crete, we discovered that Olympic Airlines was the only airline that still allowed smoking. I thought it was just an inconvenience at the time, but now I realize that it said something about the independence of the Greek spirit. I should have listened. I really should have listened.

Our tour guide boarded the bus that would take us to the cave where Zeus was born. "Good morning," she said in fluent English, "my name is Ariadne and I will be your guide." She was there again the next morning, on the bus to the ruins of the palace at Phaistos. I asked her if she was *really* Ariadne; it was just too much of a coincidence. She replied, "It's the name my mother gave me." The thread this modern Ariadne spun was made of words, stories, myth, and history; and the labyrinth she helped us thread was Crete, in all its glory and darkness.

The history of Crete is filled with oppression and resistance, with suffering and courage. Once, very long ago, Crete was a great sea power, a great artistic center, a great trading nation. Then it was overrun, first by Athenians, then by Romans, pirates, Venetian Catholics, Turkish Moslems, and Nazis. Orthodox churches became Catholic churches,

CONNECTED SPIRAL BORDER

became mosques, became Orthodox churches again. And always in the mountains there were resistance movements, Orthodox monks and farmers fighting fiercely for their faith and freedom.

Before all of that, however, Crete enjoyed one bright period, as one of the cradles of civilization. Today there is little left of the early palaces (2000–1700 BCE). Certainly, there is the great pavement at Knossos and, for me at least, it was an awe-inspiring experience to walk on stones quarried in an age before Stonehenge, before Abraham, before Gilgamesh. Still, most of the great ancient ruins of Crete come from the new palace period, shortly after 1700 BCE. These palaces were built at Malia, at Zakros, at Festos or Phaistos (transliteration from Greek to English script is not consistent on Crete), and most spectacularly at Knossos.

One can still visit the Diktean Cave high in the mountains, where Zeus is storied to have been born, as well as the ancient plane tree near Gortis, under which Zeus and Europa consummated their love. From our hotel room in Herakleion or Iraklio, we could see painted on a building a huge mural of Icarus plunging into the sea. Only three miles south of Herakleion, one can experience something of the opulence of King Minos' court at Knossos. Myth lives on Crete.

When Rome was just a gleam in Romulus' eye, and Athens was a frontier town, and Jerusalem was a Philistine hill village, the great palace of Knossos was the center of a city of 50,000 people, the capitol of an island that dominated trade in the eastern Mediterranean. Many of the rooms in the palace were decorated with frescoes, which, even today, are sophisticated, beautiful, and technically remarkable. Many delicate objects of gold and other precious metals were unearthed during the excavations. The storerooms remain full of very large jars, which still contain residues of grain, wine, olive oil, and other staples. There is even an elaborate drainage and sewer system under the palace. No wonder some scholars argue that the real labyrinth was the palace itself, with its vast network of rooms and corridors.

The story of Sir Arthur Evans' excavation of Knossos beginning in 1900 is something of a miracle. It happened during a rare window of opportunity

*Go to page 98 or 99*

GREEK KEY BORDER

between the expulsion of the Turks from Crete and the island becoming part of Greece. For a few short years, Crete existed as an independent nation and most of the treasures dug up at Knossos remain in the National Archeological Museum in Herakleion. Thus, it is possible to compare Evans' reconstructed frescoes at the site, with the originals in the museum a short bus ride away. This is important, because purists tend to be very critical of the work Evans did in an attempt to capture everyday life almost 4000 years ago. To them, the restored frescoes, reconstructed walls and pillars painted in ochres and garish reds are little better than vandalism, a valuable resource forever contaminated. Yet to my inexpert eyes, Evans' restorations were really quite modest. The original frescoes preserved in the museum in Heraklion consistently indicate what is original and what was restored. With one exception, which has since been re-restored, Evans' work seems merely to make the palace more accessible to the public, while carefully preserving and labeling all of the original bits.

I found my trip to the much smaller palace at Phaistos just as revealing. Here minimal restoration has occurred, yet many of the same features blamed on Evans can be found. For example, there are more walls standing than we have any right to expect after 3500 or more years and even where a wall *has* collapsed into rubble, it is still clear that there *was* once a wall there. The few frescoes that can be found remain amazingly fresh, though very faded, and at least as complete as most of the original frescoes from Knossos. And the colors of the pillars? They are 35-century-old faded versions of ochre and garish red. In other words, I believe that Evans has been true to the spirit of Knossos, and that entering the palace there is like stepping into a time machine.

When I got back from Crete, my minister asked me if I had found the labyrinth. It was a difficult question to answer. Certainly, I did not find a maze or labyrinth, which might have held a dangerous, cannibalistic monster. I would have been very surprised if I had. But I *did* find the remains of a labyrinthine building. As well, all of the frescoes have borders and the style of the time dictated that a variety of patterns be used. Among these patterns were the Greek key, which is still in common use, and the connected spiral. In other words, even in Minoan times Cretans used labyrinthine patterns.

As intriguing as those discoveries were for me, my pilgrimage to the home of the original labyrinth somehow gave me more than borders and the ruins of a big building. I felt that I had found the heart of the labyrinth, not by finding a physical labyrinth, but by being where it all began. I will never walk a labyrinth in quite the same way again.

Perhaps the last word on the Cretan labyrinth should belong to Sir Arthur Evans, who, according to W. H. Matthews in *Mazes and Labyrinths,* discovered deep under Knossos the entrance to an artificial cave. Evans mused, "but here, perhaps, it is better for the imagination to draw rein."

## DANCING THE LABYRINTH

I still collect books on mazes and read about mazes on the Internet, but my heart belongs to the labyrinth.

It wasn't long after my return from Crete that I led my first labyrinth workshop as part of a church study group on modes of spirituality. I used masking tape to make a walk-through Amiens labyrinth on the floor of our church's fellowship hall. The Amiens labyrinth was easier to construct than circular ones, because it only involves straight lines (see page 42). As I learned later, tape was not such a good idea. Our building superintendent told me that she had to totally strip the floor to get the adhesive off. There were only four of us at the workshop, including Joyce and me, so I did wonder whether it was worthwhile. And yet, over the following weeks, it was wonderful to watch the children walk and run and dance that labyrinth before it was finally ripped up.

This workshop led to invitations to lead other events with a women's group, a youth group, a church school class, a study group at another church. People always asked about mazes so I printed up a page with a seven-ringed Cretan labyrinth on one side, and a copy of the Hampton Court maze on the other. Half of the group would do one, half the other. Then we would talk about how we felt tracing each. Over time, I collected a set of overheads to help people understand the psychological and spiritual differences between the two.

Then, I had an opportunity to lead a group in exploring a labyrinth described as Hopi in the literature of the Native Roman Catholic center where it is situated. This labyrinth is laid out with birch logs and follows the North American Native pattern, but I quickly saw that the form is identical to the seven-ringed Cretan labyrinth. More and more, I

*Go to page 50 or 51*

was coming to realize that the labyrinth is a universal, archetypal expression of human spirituality.

Back at our church, we kept looking for a way to create our own labyrinth, which we could use whenever we wanted. We looked at canvas, at topiary, at rugs. They were too expensive or too complicated, or we did not have enough space. Then the opportunity arose for Joyce and me to work with 11- to 13-year-olds at a summer camp. We needed a labyrinth and we needed it quickly. So we bought a huge white tarpaulin and, at the expense of stiff muscles and sore knees, we had a walk-through labyrinth prepared, mostly by one person, in about eight hours. (At the end of this chapter, I will show you how to make one for yourself.)

For five days, we used this labyrinth and stories from the life of the apostle Paul to help young people understand their own journeys. We sang *One More Step Along the World I Go* and used a journeying prayer, learning a new phrase each day. We learned to draw labyrinths and we made our own labyrinth pendants and rock paperweights. A few of the kids even painted 27-ringed labyrinths on small boulders to give to their parents as garden decorations.

Every day we walked the labyrinth. On the last night, campers, counselors, and staff all joined in a sunset candlelit walk of the labyrinth. I find it difficult to describe the emotional and spiritual power of that moment. The next day, we invited the campers to go through the labyrinth in any way they saw fit, as an expression of farewell. Some walked; some crawled on their hands and knees. A couple of boys, with their own very original ideas of how to do things, crawled it on their bellies. And then there were those who danced the labyrinth.

*Dead End: Start over*

## Experience

It is not difficult to create your own large-scale, seven-ringed labyrinth; it's just time-consuming and a bit hard on the knees.

Here are the materials you'll need:

1 20' x 20' (6.1 m x 6.1 m) tarpaulin (I used white),
2 rolls of green painter's tape,
1 roll of clear parcel tape,
1 clear plastic ruler (18" or 45.7 cm is a good size),
a tape measure at least 20' (6.1 m) long,
and a marker.

If someone else is working with you, you might also want a piece of twine at least 12' (3.65 m) long.

Spread the tarpaulin out on a hard surface (I used the floor of the church basement) and tape it down so that it is taut. Find the center point at the top and bottom. Mark them with a little piece of painter's tape. You will be able to remove these when you are finished, leaving the tarpaulin unmarked. Find and mark the point 10'6" (3.2 m) from the top on the center line. Now find the point 6" (15.25 cm) to the left of that point. This will be the top of the cross. Run a 4' (1.22 m) strip of tape down from this point. At the midpoint of this tape, run another strip horizontally 2' (61 cm) in each direction. You should now have a cross with arms 2' long (61 cm), 6" (15.25 cm) below and to the left of the center.

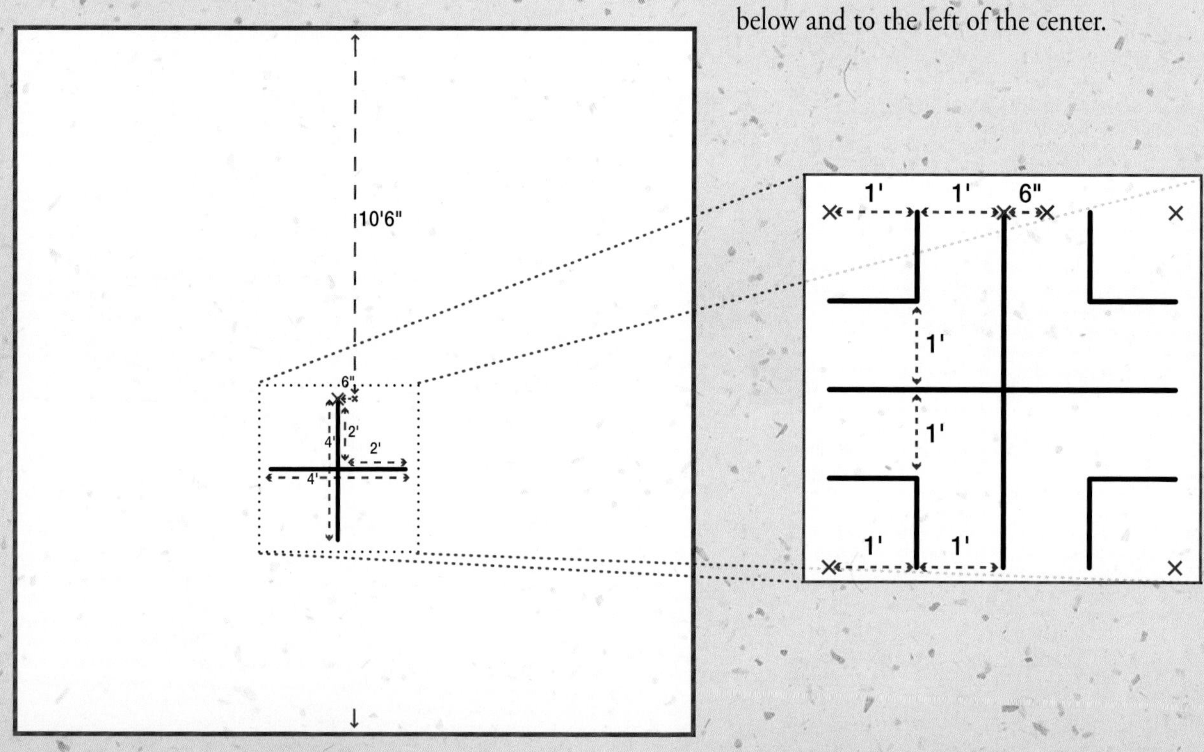


Go to page 15 or 52

Now measure and mark a point 1' (30.48 cm) to the left and right of the vertical cross bar at both the top and bottom. Run a 1' (30.48 cm) strip of tape down from the top marks and up from the bottom. Finish the four angles by running a 1' (30.48 cm) strip of tape from the end of each of these lines closest to the cross bar, making them parallel to it. Find the four points 2' (61 cm) above and below the crossbar and 2' (61 cm) to the left and right of the vertical, and mark all four. You now should have a very large version of the first step of making a seven-ringed Cretan labyrinth as outlined in Chapter 2, except that this one has a mark 6" (15.25 cm) to the right of the top of the cross.

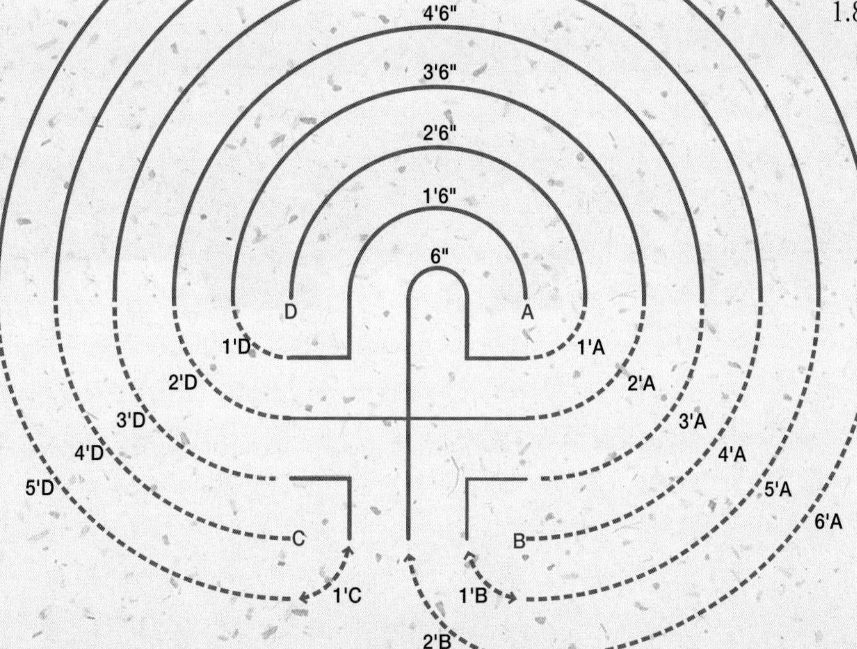


If someone is working with you, mark the twine at 6", 1'6", 2'6", 3'6", 4'6", 5'6", 6'6" and 7'6" (15.25 cm, 45.7 cm, 76 cm, 1.06 m, 1.37 m, 1.68 m, 1.98 m, and 2.29 m); and also at 1', 2', 3', 4', 5', and 6' (30.48 cm, 61 cm, 91.44 cm, 1.22 m, 1.52 m, and 1.88 m). You may now use the twine as a compass. Your partner can hold the twine at the center point, the very first point you marked, while you draw the walls of the top half of the labyrinth, indicated by solid lines in the drawing below, using the markings at 6", 1'6", 2'6", 3'6", 4'6", 5'6", 6'6", and 7'6" (15.25 cm, 45.7 cm, 76 cm, 1.06 m, 1.37 m, 1.68 m, 1.98 m, 2.29 m) on the twine. The dotted lines or bottom half of the labyrinth may be drawn centering on points A and D (for lines 1'D–5'D) and points B and C (for lines 1'B–2'B and 1'C) and using the 1', 2', 3', 4', 5', and 6' (30.48 cm, 61 cm, 91.44 cm, 1.22 m, 1.52 m, 1.88 m) markings on the twine For example, "1'A" tells you to draw a curve centered on point A, and 1' (30.48 cm) out from it. It helps to know that each of these curves indicated by dotted lines forms a quarter of a circle.

*Go to page 79 or 100*

When you have finished drawing the labyrinth, cover the drawn lines with strips of painter's tape. The tighter the curve the shorter the tape must be. For the very sweeping curves, you may use quite long strips. You will be surprised how the straight pieces of tape create the illusion of curves when the labyrinth is completed. The only problem with painter's tape is that it peels easily so you will need to cover it with strips of clear parcel tape to protect it.

If you are working alone, as I was, the process is a little more difficult. You can use your clear plastic ruler to draw the rings. Center the 0 point on the dot at the center of the labyrinth (the first point you marked) and, rotating the ruler around it, make a series of dots at the 6" (15.25 cm) point of your ruler. Next, cover the dots with little pieces of tape, thus joining the vertical arm of the cross to the line next to it. Move on to the next ring. Place the 0 point on the ring you have just made and, keeping the ruler perpendicular to the tape pieces, make a series of dots, then cover them with tape to form the next ring, and so forth. The further out you get the further apart the dots may be and the longer the strips of tape you may use.

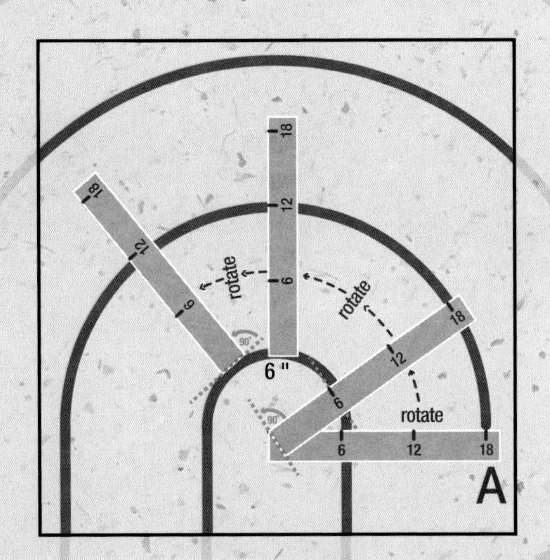


Where there are dotted lines in the diagram on page 81 you will need to center on the appropriate one of the four corner points, as described above, and use the 1' mark on the ruler. To draw lines 2'B and 2'D–5'D, you will once again need to hold the ruler perpendicular to the curve you've just draw, and mark a new curve measured 1' (30.48 cm) out.

There are two major differences if you work alone: you have to tape the curves as you go and the whole process is slower and more fiddly.

Whether you work with a friend or alone, you should be aware that, if you are in a public place as I was, you will excite curiosity and have people walking your labyrinth even before you have it finished. But that's part of the joy of making it.

When not in use, I keep my labyrinth rolled or folded up, in a large garbage bag. I also check it from time to time, as the tape may loosen and need repair; or the tarpaulin may pick up stains if it is used outdoors, and need to be cleaned.

When I am unfolding the tarpaulin for a workshop, I still feel a little thrill of accomplishment as I see the labyrinth opening up in front of me.

*Go to page 52 or 102* 

# 5

# The Maze Renewed

## Experience

Try playing a few electronic or computer games. You will quickly discover that many of them involve mazes in one way or another, and that all of them involve choices, which could be mapped onto a maze. You might find it helpful to consult a teenager about where to find the best games and, more importantly, which games you can enjoy that don't involve too much killing or too many gross images.

***The sound of the path 3:*** The dissonance, complexity, and challenge of much 20th-century music would be a very suitable accompaniment to working the mazes in this chapter. My own favorite composer of this period is Stravinsky, especially his *Rite of Spring.* But many composers would be equally good; the atonality of much of Schönberg, for example; or the jagged, urban sounds of Gershwin's *Slaughter on 10th Avenue,* would help reflect the complex, almost industrial quality of these mazes. If you enjoy rock music or heavy metal, then use that. Experimental popular music like the Beatles' *Revolution #9* would also be appropriate. There are even some explicitly religious works, such as Olivier Messiaen's *Quartette for the End of Time,* that are so challenging that they would go well with these implicitly secular mazes. Choose music that you enjoy. Or perhaps, better still, choose music that you don't particularly enjoy, but that challenges you.

See if you can draw a map of the maze in one of the games you experimented with.

*Go to page 54 or 55*

## TO BEGIN WITH

The maze never really died; it simply went into a latency period, waiting for its puberty and the opportunity to come back in a more mature form. There were always a few mazes around: occasional story mazes in children's magazines, occasional timed mazes in adult crossword magazines, occasional mirror mazes at carnivals. Then, something happened. Today, when I enter the word "maze" into my Internet search engine, I am offered over 1,600,000 sites. Without a doubt, the maze has come back.

Though many of the mazes discussed in this chapter are paper or walk-through mazes, the explosion of interest in the maze really began and is deeply rooted in the computer. What the computer contributed to the maze was complexity – not just complexity, but complexity upon complexity.

MIRROR MAZE, LONGLEAT, WILTSHIRE, UK

*Go to page 83 or 104*

## The Electronic Maze

The resurgence of the maze can be traced to two phenomena from the 1960s and the early 1970s: role-playing games and programmed texts.

The most successful of all role-playing games is *Dungeons and Dragons,* which has spawned books and films and computer games, as well as dozens of imitators, most of which don't match the excitement of the original. In "D&D," one player takes on the role of the dungeon master. She or he designs an adventure for the other players, who take on the roles of various supernatural creatures and who try to win their way through a maze of obstacles and monsters, which confront them on their journey. The dungeon is often a very complex maze of some sort. The game depends on the ingenuity of the dungeon master and the imaginative visualization of the players.

Even though she oversimplified the psychology of gamers, Rona Jaffe showed that she understood the role of mazes in gaming when she called her novel about the subject *Mazes and Monsters.*

It was a small step from the imagination of a dungeon master to the innards of a computer. The binary either/or electronic structure of computer programming and language almost perfectly mimics choice in a maze. Mazes also have the virtue of taking relatively little computer memory. Thus, the computer game was born. Electronic games are nothing but portable computer games. As graphics become more and more realistic, the computer can take us through all sorts of maze adventures that require minimal use of our imaginations.

All of these adventures depend on a set of choices, which could be mapped with maze-like patterns, and many of them actually take place within mazes.

In the late 1960s, programmed texts became a fashion among educators. The programmed text was modeled on computer-directed learning. The program required the learner to make choices. Incorrect answers returned the learner to pages where the material had been taught. These loops allowed learners to cover the same material over and over again until it was mastered. Computer-directed learning operated in exactly the same way, with loops repeating content until it was mastered. Programmed texts and computer-directed learning can be a very effective way to learn content quickly. For example, I once needed to master probability theory very quickly. An hour a day with a programmed text met my need in a few weeks.

*Go to page 56 or 86*

The form of the programmed text is exactly the same as the form of later book mazes, for example, *Maze,* by Christopher Manson. *Maze* presents a house with 42 rooms. Each room is illustrated on its own page. Its facing page carries the story of the journey through that room. Entering the first room, the reader may choose to go to room 20, room 26, room 41, or room 21. If the reader chooses to go to room 20, he or she will find doors to room 5, room 37, room 27, or back to room 1. The goal is to get from room 1 to room 45, then back to room 1 going through the smallest number of rooms possible. There are many visual clues and other puzzles to be solved along the way. This is a fiercely difficult maze and a prize was offered to the first person who solved it.

Turn to page 98 of this book to experience a book maze based on programmed texts.

## MAZES FOR CHILDREN

There are still many examples of old-fashioned mazes for children around. However, during the last 30 years, children's mazes have become so sophisticated that it is hard to distinguish them from mazes intended for adults.

A typical early children's maze book is Walter Shepherd's *Big Book of Mazes & Labyrinths,* from 1973. In contains many traditional story mazes. Quite a few of the mazes present modest complications – collecting letters to spell words; avoiding obstacles, such as a London bobby (police officer); finding the shortest path. However, these are only modest additions to the difficulty of mazes that children would have found elsewhere.

*3-Dimensional Monster Mazes,* by Larry Evans, appears to be aimed at children, with its mildly scary spiders and snakes, and its rather cute caterpillar eating its way through Dracula's cape to emerge as a butterfly. Yet the level of difficulty is not much less than his adult three-dimensional mazes. In fact, many of these so-called children's mazes are just his adult mazes populated by ghosts or aliens or the dreaded bramble beast. The mazes in this 1976 book are considerably more difficult than most in Shepherd's *Big Book.*

Rolf Heimann's 1989 book, *Amazing Mazes,* puts a whole different twist on children's mazes. The book features the adventures of three children and is

clearly aimed at children, even though the author says in his subtitle that they are "for ages 6-60." There are many different sorts of puzzles in this book, but its core is made up of 12 relatively simple story mazes. Heimann complicates these puzzles by presenting a different problem for each of the three children. Thus, what begins as a simple maze becomes much more complex, as each of the three paths weaves through, over, and around one another.

In 1999, Richard Burne published a series of quite demanding mazes for children in *Masterpath.* Each maze is based on some historical event: the building of the Sphinx, Napoleon's retreat from Moscow, the embarkation of Christopher Columbus. Each is illustrated with meticulous detail, especially in the elaborate architecture and the dozens of people who inhabit the pictures. My personal favorite has Florence Nightingale finding her way through the darkened hospital at Scutari, in order to break up the partying of a group of nurses and patients. The art is clearly aimed at children, but very bright children they would have to be.

It appears from developments in children's maze books that children must be getting smarter. Whether or not this is so, they are surely getting more savvy at navigating mazes of ever increasing complexity. This is not surprising. Children who can master the much more complicated mazes of electronic and computer games would be bored by the old puzzles that charmed me as a child. They want and need to do more than get the bunny safely home by avoiding the fox and the stoat (whatever a stoat may be).

## ULTRAMAZES FOR ADULTS

In mazes designed for adults during this same period (about 1970 to the present), we encounter what I call the "ultramaze." Ultramazes go beyond the old hedge mazes, making a statement by being the biggest, or the most dramatic, or the most fabulous, or the most difficult, or the most unlikely maze ever designed. That is, until the next one, which is even bigger, even more dramatic…

The age of the ultramaze was initiated in the early 1970s by Greg Bright, who designed and installed a huge hedge maze at Longleat House, the home of the Marquis of Bath. This maze opened to the public in 1978 and boasts complex spiral junctions (an innovation), six bridges (another innovation), and the longest distance in paths of any hedge maze in the world. In short, Bright initiated a revolution in maze design.

*Go to page 60 or 88*

Panel Maze at Planets, East Tawas, Michigan

In New Zealand and in Australia, and later in Japan, wooden panel mazes were developed that were even longer and larger than the Longleat maze. They also contained bridges and, occasionally, underground passages joining different parts of the maze. In Japan, these mazes became a craze. Between 1985 and 1990, 200 were built, each bigger and more complicated than the last. Some had the capacity to process up to 1500 people an hour. Even though today the fad has been replaced by other attractions, some wooden panel mazes remain around the Pacific Rim – from Japan to Australia to California – and they remain popular.

*Go to page 106 or 107*

The Longleat House Maze

*Go to page 91 or 107*

Today the craze for "maize mazes" in North America parallels the craze for wooden panel mazes in Japan during the late 1980s. Farmers are creating maze patterns in their grain crops, and then opening them to the public in order to supplement their income. Hundreds of these mazes are made each year, often increasing in difficulty year by year.

I once walked a relatively easy corn maze just outside of London, Ontario, and can attest that corn makes a wonderful maze, especially when it has grown "as high as an elephant's eye." Like the earlier wooden puzzle mazes, these maize mazes are introducing the joys of the maze to many people, who might never have encountered them in books.

Adrian Fisher and his associates, first with Minotaur Designs and later with Adrian Fisher Designs, have to be given the credit for the most original, the most personal, and the downright prettiest mazes being created. In their designs, they attempt to reflect the character of the people for whom they are working. Fisher's 1981 Archbishop's Maze, for example, is both a maze and a labyrinth and can be walked as either. The maze is based on a dream of the Archbishop of Canterbury, which became the basis of his enthronement sermon; the labyrinth is one of several Christian symbols woven ingeniously into the maze. Other examples of Fisher's work include The Lappa Valley Railway Maze, which

*Go to page 92 or 118*

is patterned on an antique steam engine, and the Beatles' Maze in Liverpool, which was shaped like an apple and wended its way through a yellow submarine. Fisher mazes are not particularly difficult, but he has brought humor and charm and personality to the field.

Fisher, with Howard Loxton, has recently published a book called *Secrets of the Maze.* This is a wonderful source for maze designs, especially hedge mazes. The authors must have thought that their readers would not find ordinary hedge maze designs challenging enough, because they have layered a second puzzle over most of them to make them more difficult. They have added treasures to be collected to the Hampton Court maze, directional arrows to the Chevening House maze, dice representing tunnels to the Chatsworth House maze, and so forth. Here we see in a small way an example of the ever increasing mania for more and more complexity in adult mazes.

I have already mentioned Larry Evans' three-dimensional mazes. These had paths or roads that wound over and under one another, or were embedded in fantastic land- or cityscapes, or represented vast systems of pipes. Ultimately, it would seem, Evans must have tired of the limitations of mazes the size of the pages of a book, because he went on to produce three mazes in the format of 25" x 27" posters: *Giant 3Dimensional Maze, The Largest 3Dimensional Maze in the Universe,* and *The Most Gigantic 3Dimensional Maze in the Galaxy.* The latter does seem a slight exaggeration. These mazes are huge versions of his usual three-dimensional themes: a prince rescuing a maiden, a complicated mass of pipes, the winding throughways and cloverleaves towering over and around a futuristic city. What is original is the sheer size and complexity of his poster mazes.

David Pelham has gone beyond Evans in the creation of three-dimensional mazes. Evans was satisfied to represent the third dimension on the page. Pelham has created the pop-up maze in his book *Dimensional Mazes.* These are not large mazes, but they are very difficult to solve because of the various layers and shapes that emerge as part of the pop-up form. Some of Pelham's mazes add to the confusion with flaps that change the configuration of the paths depending on which side of the flap is showing. One wonders what the next step in three-dimensional mazes will be. Holographic mazes?

*The Ultimate Maze Book* is published by Guinness Superlatives Ltd. and features these words prominently: "WARNING THIS BOOK CAN SERIOUSLY DAMAGE YOUR BRAIN." It is filled with very large (11.5" x 16.5"), but, ultimately, traditional mazes. They are solvable with time and effort.

*Go to page 92 or 108*

Some mazes seem to me to be unsolvable. Consider Dave Phillips' *The World's Most Difficult Maze.* There's no hyperbole this time. It really is that difficult. The maze occupies the entire book, 28 pages. It begins on page 4 and winds its way all the way to page 31. First you have to be following the correct path; then you have to find the correct "ingenious" hole to get to the next page. There are up to seven holes through each page giving you access to the next, only one of them correct. No, I've never solved it, nor do I think I will ever be able to. One of the mazes at the end of this chapter is modeled on Phillips' maze, but it's only four pages long and uses a simpler method than holes to get from one page to another.

## IN THE SPIRIT OF THE TIMES

It is easier to look back and recognize the spirituality of other times than to see the spirituality of our own times. Typically, our own worldview is almost invisible to us, because it usually appears to us as simple common sense. By comparison, the worldviews of other cultures and other times appear to be exotic, and are therefore recognizable in their distinctness. However, by examining changes in the nature of our symbols, we may see our own spirituality more objectively. Changes in the role, construction, and interpretation of mazes, for example, open a window on changes that have been occurring in our basic values. In effect, the maze becomes a barometer registering changes in society's basic beliefs.

The most obvious change is that new for-profit mazes are being developed on private property. Early mazes were created on private land for the amusement of the wealthy and their friends. But by Victorian times, during the Gothic revival, hedge mazes were planted in public gardens, primarily for families to enjoy free of charge, though those in amusement parks and tea gardens had admission fees. As late as the 1960s and early 1970s, free public mazes, such as the Bath Centennial Maze and the Toronto Island Centennial Maze, were still being constructed. This changed completely in the 1970s, when the Marquis of Bath installed Greg Bright's huge hedge maze as part of the development of his estate as a profit-making theme park. At Longleat, one pays to enter the grounds and pays again to enter the maze. Since then, private maze construction has become the norm. The huge wooden panel mazes found around the Pacific Rim were all built by corporations in the entertainment industry. Maize mazes are meant to supplement farmers' incomes, or to attract customers to buy produce, or both. This change points to a significant change in the spirit of the times.

*Go to page 89 or 107*

For much of society, there exists an underlying, almost religious belief in private, for-profit enterprise. In most countries, a great deal of public policy is based on this premise. Private health care, education, welfare, etc., are promoted as a matter of unquestionable principle. Critics of this policy of privatization of essential services say that private greed is being fostered at the expense of the public good. Advocates say that competition fosters efficiency. They argue that anyone should be able to profit from whatever they do, even if it's only creating mazes. Why should maze entrepreneurs and entertainment corporations and farmers have to compete with free, publicly sponsored mazes?

As a symbol, the maze also speaks to the innovation, invention, and rapid change that define our age. In months, sometimes in weeks, technology becomes outdated, but not technology alone. Fashions, entertainment, food, relationships, even religion: almost everything in life changes with head-spinning rapidity. The maze reflects this passion for novelty. Greg Bright introduced two new elements in the maze at Longleat House: bridges and spirals, both of which became standard in subsequent mazes. Up until that time, even though every maze was different, there were quite standard patterns that applied to all mazes and a limited variety of materials from which mazes were made: hedges, paper and ink, glass and mirrors. After 1978, creators of mazes began using many new materials and introducing many new elements into their patterns. Wood, plastic, and grain, and, especially, electronic circuitry, became common materials for the construction of mazes. Computers made it possible to travel through mazes that could never be built in the real world. Letters, numbers, shapes, colors, and directional arrows became common in printed mazes. Overlapping mazes were printed on the same page. Mazes popped up from the page or cut down through it. Eventually, whole books were printed that consisted of a single maze. The story of the maze over the last 30 years reflects the increasing value that much of society puts on novelty.

Society has been deeply divided by the increasing emphasis put on secularity, novelty, and privatization as ultimate values. In the next chapter, we will see the reaction against these values from a more religious perspective and the way in which the labyrinth has become an important symbol of this resistance. But whether we see the world in secular terms or religious terms, whether we believe in private rights or the public good, whether we crave tradition or novelty, one inescapable fact of the Western world today is its increasing complexity, confusion, and complicatedness – and this is perfectly symbolized by the increasing complexity and difficulty of the maze.

I do not believe that most maze designers and maze enthusiasts consciously connect the increasing complexity of mazes with the increasing complexity of life in our modern world. But symbols are most

*Go to page 92 or 109*

powerful when they are created and experienced through the subconscious. "Deep speaks unto deep." Myth resonates at our most basic level, without our necessarily being aware that it is myth that calls out to us.

Complex mazes appeal to us, I believe, because they speak deep within us of the difficulty of finding our way in life today. The old certainties no longer seem so certain. "Get an education and you'll get a good job." "Anyone can get ahead if they work hard." "Save for a rainy day." Of course, these clichés were never universally true, but today they seem open to challenge. Good jobs evaporate suddenly; luck seems more important than effort; savings can be wiped out by somebody else's bad investment. Life is risky in this increasingly complicated world. Multinational organizations of various kinds make it very difficult to assign blame when things go wrong. Globalization makes it very difficult to know where and when the most important decisions in our lives are being made. Confusing bureaucratic rules grow like weeds in all organizations. Life is a maze.

That metaphor "life is a maze" is certainly reflected on the Internet. Of the over one and a half million sites for "maze," about half of them use the term metaphorically. Here are just a few examples:

- Through the Maze – an anti-Mormon site
- Micromercurial Maze – concerning dental amalgams
- The Resurrection Maze – about contradictions in the Gospel accounts
- Through the Maze – information services
- The Moral Maze
- Running the Liberal Hate Maze – a reactionary rant
- Negotiating the Special Education Maze
- Navigating the Maze of Criminal Records Retrieval
- Navigating the Patent Maze
- Navigating the Mortgage Maze
- Navigating the Maze of Sunscreens

Internet sites that refer to the maze in a metaphorical sense exist in the hundreds of thousands. In contrast, there are very few sites that refer to the labyrinth in a metaphorical way; most refer to actual labyrinths. I believe that the increasing complexity of actual mazes reflects metaphorically the increasing complexity of so many dimensions of life. Mazes have become embodied metaphor.

## Experience

The recent mazes discussed in this chapter have become incredibly complex. I find that they are more curiosities or works of art and ingenuity than puzzles to actually be solved. They represent the complexity of modern life where decisions often have to be made without many of the variables being known.

The four puzzles in this experience, each in a different way, present samples of the problems we find in modern mazes, in that the tricks for solving mazes won't usually work for them. We can't put a hand on the wall, because there are islands or else there are no walls to put a hand on. We can't begin at the end, because it may not be clear just where the end is, or tracing back may lead somewhere else than the beginning. We can't glance ahead or back, because often we can only see part of the puzzle at a time. So here are four puzzle mazes for you to explore. But be warned! Each is more diabolical than the one before it.

1. ***The three-dimensional maze***
   You enter and exit the maze on this page by the same path in the upper right-hand corner. Paths cross over and under one another, so when you come to what looks like a dead end you will always be able to continue on the other side of the intervening path. You must follow the arrows. If you come up against an arrowhead pointing the opposite way, you must turn around and go back. The good news is that there are no dead ends. The bad news is that there are lots of endless loops. If you get stuck in one and can't get out, you just have to start again. This one is really not all that difficult.

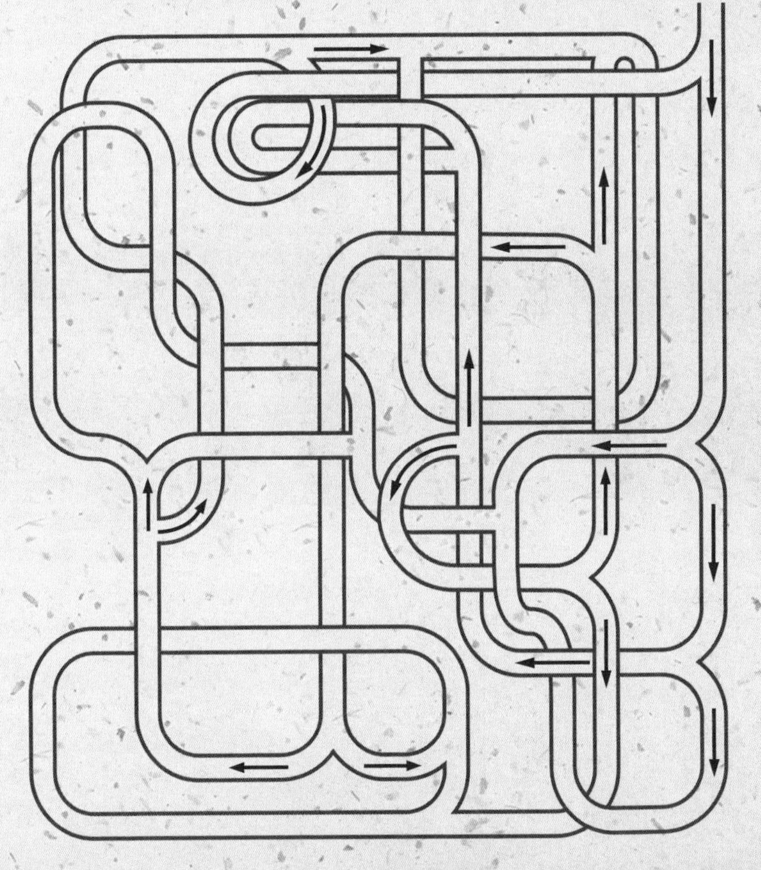

*Go to page 94 or 111*

2. ***The letter maze***
   On page 97, begin at any of the 12 corners; they are marked by arrows. Only one of them will allow you to solve the puzzle. Move from letter to letter horizontally or vertically but never diagonally. You will find that you can form words, which, if you are on the correct path, will eventually form a delightful quotation. This maze ends at the large center square, which you can reach from any of the 12 adjacent squares. You may write down the words as go, or, for a more difficult maze, keep them in your mind. There is only one correct solution. Watch out for false leads; there are many of them. Simpler versions of letter mazes are sometimes found in crossword magazines. Letter mazes of this complexity are printed in some maze books.

3. ***The multipage maze***
   This maze runs from pages 98 to 101. The start and finish are adjacent on the first page. On page 99/100, you will find a dotted line. Trim off the outer edge of the page by cutting along this line; the page should now be 1" narrower than the rest of the pages in this book. Some paths on page 99 match paths on page 101 and some paths on page 100 match paths on page 98. You will work back and forth from one page to another to solve this maze.

4. ***The book maze*** This book is a maze! No doubt you have noticed the notations that appear at the bottom corner of each page. Well, they are all part of an elaborate maze, which you can now ***begin by going to one of the page options given at the bottom of this page.*** Starting with one of these three numbers (already you have to make a choice), follow the page numbers to find your way to ***THE END.***

***TIP: Watch out for endless loops and dead ends. Since you're dealing with one page at a time, they are difficult to predict and avoid.***

*Go to page 41, 97 or 119* 

A Letter Maze

| I | T | S | H | E | R | E | T | T | A | | | | | | N | O | T | R | E | A | O | R | R | A |
|---|---|---|---|---|---|---|---|---|---|---|---|---|---|---|---|---|---|---|---|---|---|---|---|---|
| T | W | R | T | T | H | G | H | A | R | | | | | | E | S | T | U | D | D | F | Y | A | M |
| I | L | I | H | U | L | U | A | T | I | | | | | | E | E | U | N | A | A | O | R | R | E |
| S | F | F | E | O | D | N | O | E | A | | | | | | R | I | X | D | M | M | M | A | E | P |
| E | O | E | S | C | N | T | T | N | D | | | | | | T | L | S | E | D | A | O | B | R | X |
| C | N | A | E | Y | E | B | F | I | N | W | E | Z | A | X | R | A | N | C | E | Z | F | A | D | E |
| V | E | D | U | E | H | T | Q | U | D | A | A | F | M | E | H | T | A | O | R | Y | A | L | A | N |
| D | H | T | S | M | A | T | E | P | E | W | N | D | T | H | I | T | D | E | Z | A | M | A | D | A |
| E | L | T | I | C | Z | U | B | O | B | A | Y | R | O | E | L | A | A | T | R | D | A | P | E | H |
| C | E | L | T | S | E | S | E | N | A | S | T | H | U | R | Y | B | N | H | D | A | D | A | H | I |
| | | | | | N | A | R | T | P | A | C | A | G | A | S | Y | D | E | R | | | | | |
| | | | | | E | R | U | N | R | C | | | | Z | I | R | S | R | A | | | | | |
| | | | | | S | E | C | E | E | O | | H | | T | N | C | U | E | W | | | | | |
| | | | | | T | H | M | E | D | L | | | | I | D | H | A | C | E | | | | | |
| | | | | | R | T | O | T | P | A | T | E | V | D | T | A | S | E | R | | | | | |
| A | L | A | B | Y | A | I | G | E | I | N | W | R | E | E | W | S | O | T | A | P | L | A | R | S |
| M | E | H | E | R | O | T | H | S | O | L | C | Y | L | I | P | E | M | L | A | W | T | I | I | P |
| A | Z | T | D | I | S | E | W | I | J | H | M | E | P | O | E | L | E | K | U | K | E | R | I | P |
| T | H | S | N | O | Y | E | G | N | I | T | A | E | L | P | B | A | N | T | T | A | O | K | M | S |
| N | I | P | E | R | F | B | E | D | W | N | T | N | I | R | Y | D | V | E | N | C | F | T | H | E |
| I | N | R | E | A | D | E | M | O | W | | | | | | B | A | A | C | S | E | Z | A | M | D |
| R | Y | B | A | S | S | D | E | V | A | | | | | | A | N | A | O | T | H | L | S | A | N |
| C | U | T | L | E | B | A | R | O | F | | | | | | L | K | B | C | E | G | A | H | T | N |
| N | O | S | R | Z | E | F | O | R | Y | | | | | | A | L | C | O | M | U | B | Y | R | I |
| A | T | H | E | A | M | E | T | I | M | | | | | | W | E | L | G | U | O | H | T | L | A |

*Go to page 74 or 75*

*Go to page 74 or 97*

Go to page 75 or 98

Dead End: Start over

*Go to page 79 or 100*

Were you able to solve these mazes? What was it like working on them? Was it fun? Confusing? Frustrating? Did you get a sense that these mazes reflected something of the complexity and confusion of the modern world? Would you choose to collect mazes like this? Why or why not? Why do you think other people create them? Why do you think other people buy them? Do they speak to the spirit of our times? If so, how? Think about the differences in feeling in solving these complex mazes, as opposed to following a labyrinth. Does this difference tell you anything about yourself?

In case you are wondering, the quotation in the letter maze is from the 1980 enthronement speech of the Rev. Dr. Robert Runcie, Archbishop of Canterbury.

Solutions to these four mazes can be found on page 125.

Winter Soltice Sun Touching the Standing Stone, Newgrange, UK

*Go to page 100 or 114*

# 6

# The Labyrinth Renewed

## EXPERIENCE

The first part of this chapter is about the use of the labyrinth within the New Age spiritual movement, as one of many tools to experience the spiritual dimension of life. As you walk or trace the labyrinths in this book, or other labyrinths that you have found, you might like to focus on one or more of the central themes of New Age spirituality. These include spirit (sometimes called energy), unity, peace, ecology, the feminine, and healing.

***The sound of the path 4.*** The obvious music to play with these experiences is "New Age" music. However, it's not to everyone's taste, because it tends to be soothing background music for meditation. This, to my mind, is what makes it suitable; but, for many people, if music does not make a strong statement, it quickly becomes irritating. An alternative to New Age music would be "world music." The pan pipe, the sitar, the Celtic harp, or even the dulcimer, might provide a satisfying accompaniment to the labyrinth used as a New Age spiritual tool.

*Go to page 54 or 120*

Another alternative would be classical music that has been recorded with natural sounds. Such albums have names like *Debussy in the Garden* and *Ravel by the Seashore.* Their intent is to be calming and relaxing, which makes them perfect for some people for New Age meditations.

Ask yourself whether this experience of tracing the labyrinth differs from any earlier experiences you may have had with it. If so, how? If not, is it because all of this was already implicit in your earlier experiences?

If you have a walk-through labyrinth available, try dancing it. A group of people could dance it in a chain, holding hands and using one of the patterns of sacred dance. If you dance it alone, move freely, expressing your full self in movement. What is it like for you to dance the labyrinth alone? Did you gain any new insights? What is it like to dance it with a group? Try discussing with the group what it was like for each of them. Did you learn anything about your own experience by doing this?

## To Begin With

By the 1970s, many people had become disillusioned with organized religion. Rightly or wrongly, they felt that it had become more interested in having more dollars in the bank and more people in the pews, than in the spiritual depth of its adherents. The disaffected no longer found stories about someone else's experience of the holy satisfying; they wanted their own experience. The rediscovery of the labyrinth, first within the New Age Movement, then within the Church, is one little chapter within the much larger story – the story of the rediscovery of personal spirituality.

A major theme of this book has been understanding the labyrinth as a spiritual symbol that points to mystery. The labyrinth's meaning is never completely understood and its origins are shrouded in the mists of prehistory. So it seems surprising that we know so much about the events surrounding the revival of interest in the labyrinth. The North American church's reclaiming of the labyrinth as a specifically Christian symbol stems from Lauren Artress' visit to Chartres, in March of 1991. But more general spiritual use of the labyrinth can readily be traced to the 1979 publication of Geoffrey Ashe's *The Glastonbury Tor Maze.* So we begin at Glastonbury.

*Go to page 82, 83 or 116*

## THE GLASTONBURY LABYRINTH

The town of Glastonbury in Somerset, England, has become one of the world's major centers for New Age spirituality. This is because many ancient legends cling to it and because of the mysterious, mythic quality of its landscape.

Glastonbury Tor is both a literal, modern hill, and the mythic Avalon. It can be seen from a great distance because of the flat Somerset Lowlands, from which it suddenly rises. Legend says that in ancient times these lowlands were flooded and that the Tor, along with two lower neighboring hills, Chalice Hill and Wearyall (or Wirrial) Hill, formed the Isle of Avalon, so important to the legends of King Arthur. Today there are gravesites on the grounds of the ruins of Glastonbury Abbey, where Arthur and Guenevere are supposed to have been buried (though several other locations claim the same privilege).

Even more significant are the Christian legends attached to Glastonbury. Most of them relate to Joseph of Arimathea, an actual New Testament

GLASTONBURY TOR

*Go to page 86 or 87*

figure. One story says that he brought the Virgin Mary and the boy Jesus to Glastonbury, after the death of Mary's husband, a different Joseph. William Blake wrote a poem called *Jerusalem* about this, which has become a very popular hymn. It begins:

And did those feet in ancient time
walk upon England's mountains green?
And was the holy Lamb of God
on England's pleasant pastures seen?

Another story has gained more credence. It is told that after the death and resurrection of Jesus, Joseph of Arimathea was forced to leave Jerusalem because he had provided Jesus' burial place. He fled first to Marseille, France. There the local bishop commissioned him to go to England, where he founded the first church in Britain, at Glastonbury.

When he landed at Glastonbury, he followed a row of oaks up onto the hills. Two of these oaks still exist, named for two kings who would one day invade Israel according to prophecy: Gog and Magog. These trees are ancient and gnarled and look half dead. Anyone seeing them today could easily believe that they are 2000 years old. Perhaps they really are.

Joseph's crossing had been grueling and he collapsed on Wearyall Hill, shoving his staff into the ground. When he awoke, the staff had taken root and was blossoming. This became the famous Glastonbury thorn, which is said to bloom twice a year, at Christmas and at Easter. During the civil war in the 1640s, it was chopped down by a Puritan soldier because it smacked of popery and superstition. It is said that this soldier was blinded by a flying chip. Fortunately, many cuttings had been planted in other places and the Glastonbury thorn was soon restored to Wearyall Hill, where it flourishes today.

Glastonbury has appropriately been called the mother of legend.

In 1968, Geoffrey Russell suggested in an article that the ridges on Glastonbury Tor actually formed a labyrinth. Geoffrey Ashe, a Glastonbury resident and Arthurian scholar, spent ten years investigating and, in 1979, published *The Glastonbury Tor Maze,* in which he presented a detailed map of the maze (actually a labyrinth). When I was in Glastonbury in 1989, a path was beginning to be worn by the feet of tourists like myself, but it was not that clear just where it went. I understand that there is now a clearer labyrinthine path up the tor to the little medieval chapel at its summit. If we believe that Glastonbury Tor forms a labyrinth, and the evidence is mounting, it is by far the largest labyrinth in the world.

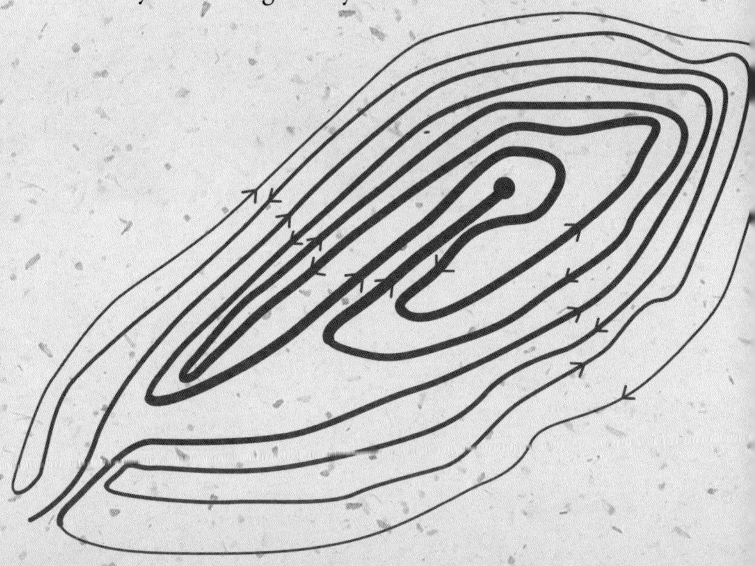

*Go to page 105 or 107*

## THE NEW AGE LABYRINTH

The New Age Movement is a catchall term for a new interest in spirituality that emerged in the 1970s. It began as a sort of underground movement that gradually became mainstream, ultimately finding its way into organized religion. But at the beginning, its roots lay in some people's rejection of what they perceived as the sterility of organized religion; they needed their own personal, direct experience of the spiritual. And so they mined the religions of the world for techniques that would allow them to have such experiences; they turned to science and to the secret, esoteric traditions. Out of all of this, a sort of folk theology was forged. At its core was the idea that the physical universe is an expression of the more real spiritual universe. (They often use the word "energy" to mean the spiritual basis of all that is.) There is a unity to everything because everything is an expression of spirit or energy. We can "see the universe in a grain of sand" or vice versa. As G. A. Studdert Kennedy wrote, "Even tumble bugs and angleworms have soul/there's soul in everything that squirms." Only he didn't go far enough; there's soul in everything that doesn't squirm, too.

SISTERS OF ST. JOSEPH MOTHER HOUSE LABYRINTH, NORTH BAY, ONTARIO

*Dead End: Start over*

To help us get in touch with this energy, this spirit, this soul, the New Age Movement uses techniques from religious and other sources. Buddhist meditation, Sufi dance, Cherokee drumming, Gregorian chant, Vedic meditation all become legitimate techniques to put us in touch with energy. When I first encountered this, I found it difficult because of my training in religious studies, which emphasizes the integrity of each religious tradition. Is it really possible to wrench a method free of its history and theology and use it for a different purpose?

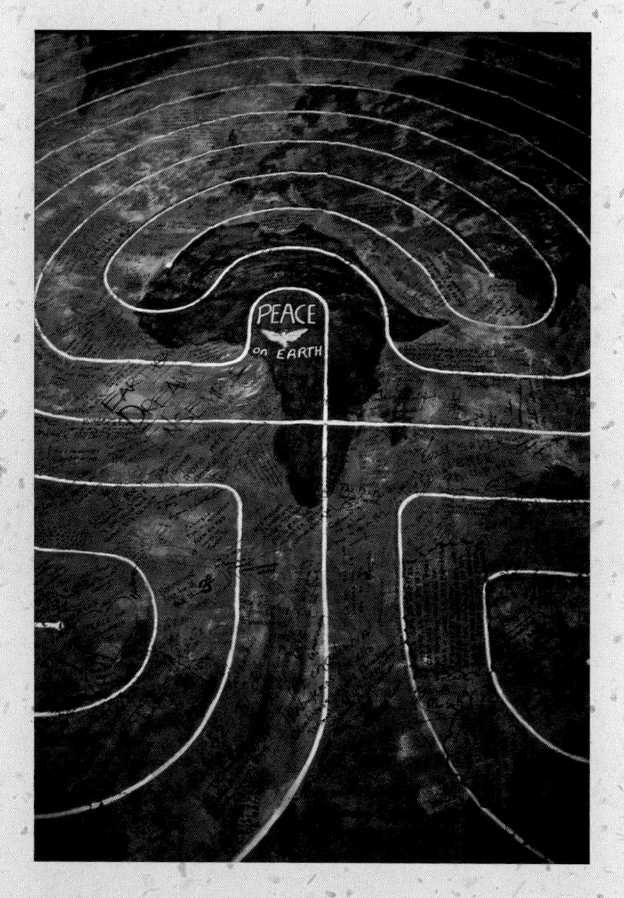


World Peace Canvas Labyrinth

What about the years of training and indoctrination necessary for the use of these religious techniques within the context of their own traditions? I consulted William Bloom, a leading English thinker in the New Age Movement, with a PhD from the prestigious London School of Economics. His response was typical. "If it works, why wouldn't you use it? If it doesn't work, forget it." During a year in England and Scotland studying the Movement, I found this very practical attitude everywhere.

I realize that not everyone will be comfortable with everything in the New Age Movement; there is much in it with which *I* am uncomfortable. It has sometimes been exploited by unscrupulous people; it has sometimes trivialized insights of science and of the great religious traditions. But all religions have had their bad moments. The New Age Movement needs to be taken seriously and understood. It expresses a spiritual hunger and a hunger for real religious experience, which many people feel. I have tried to describe its use of and beliefs about labyrinths, below, as objectively as possible so that you can make your own judgments.

The labyrinth was a technique just waiting to be used in the New Age Movement. One group within the Movement was the dowsers. Dowsers have come a long way since men with forked sticks looked for wells. Today they use high-tech metal rods and pendulums to try to discern various types of earth energies, or to locate water and minerals. But the basis is the same; the tools enhance their intuition to find energies. In the 1970s, dowsers began to spread

*Go to page 89 or 107*

sand labyrinths on the floor at their conventions. The energy created by the labyrinth allowed them to test their rods and pendulums under controlled conditions.

Using energy for healing is another part of the New Age Movement. Healing is about restoring wholeness, though not always about curing. It was quickly discovered that the energy created by labyrinths promoted healing in this sense and labyrinths began to be used at healing workshops and by private healers. It was a small step to the installation of labyrinths in wellness centers and hospitals: for example, the stone labyrinth on the grounds of the Provena Wellness Center, in Elgin, Illinois.

Many New Age practitioners believe in reincarnation. For them, the labyrinth symbolizes death and rebirth. The heart of the labyrinth is the womb and the energy of the labyrinth is decidedly feminine. The transformative power of the labyrinth is rooted in this feminine imagery, or, as in Helen Raphael Sands' *The Healing Labyrinth,* in the interaction between the masculine and the feminine. Sands goes on to say that later labyrinths with "open, empty" centers, like the one at Saffron Walden, actually transcend this interaction to create a "womb of hope." Feminine energy, so long suppressed in Western patriarchal society, needs to be re-experienced as a basis for healing.

One emphasis in the New Age Movement closely related to healing is peace. For example, at Findhorn, a New Age retreat center in the north of Scotland, meditations which focus on peace are

held twice daily. There was no labyrinth at Findhorn when I was there in 1989, but in many other retreat centers the labyrinth meditation is dedicated to peace, in the form of healing both personal relationships and national animosities. Moreover, many New Age practitioners believe that labyrinths can focus ley lines and other earth energies, which can help us to understand how to restore ecological balance to our damaged planet. So the peace that labyrinth energies represent, includes interspecies peace and even a healing of the earth in all its fullness.

The New Age Movement is important in itself. It is also important because it was a wake-up call to organized religion. Many churches realized that they had been neglecting the spiritual and the experiential, and genuine renewal is now happening as a result – renewal which has, as we shall see, found its own uses for the labyrinth.

*Go to page 66 or 106*

# The Art of the Labyrinth

Since 1987, when Alex Champion was inspired to begin creating huge earthwork labyrinth installations, dozens of artists have made variations on the labyrinth. In addition, we do not know how many ordinary people have built their own labyrinths in their homes or yards, usually following the Cretan or Chartres design. The number must be in the thousands by now.

Many artists' labyrinths are very experimental in nature. In Austrian artist Marianne Ewaldt's installation, "Ariadne's Thread," we follow a winding, bright red rope instead of paths.
In Scotland, Jim Buchanan created a sand labyrinth at low tide. As the tide came in, first the paths filled with water; then the entire labyrinth disappeared; as the tide went out, the beach was wiped smooth. A similar, even more temporary pattern was created by England's Chris Parsons. At dawn, on a bowling green, he brushed the labyrinthine pattern into the dew, which evaporated with the rising sun.

Almost any material and method can be used by the homeowner to create a personal labyrinth. Probably one of the easiest is cropping a grass path in deeper grass, like the one at Holy Trinity Church, in Toronto. However, bricks, paving stones, wood chips, wood, sand, tiles and a host of other materials – almost anything you can think of – have been used by someone somewhere. Fountains have been created that follow labyrinth patterns. Labyrinths have been created for the bottom of ponds or even swimming pools. Labyrinth tiles, woven hangings, and carpets, like the one at Grace Cathedral in San Francisco, have been made to be traced with fingers, to decorate walls, and to be walked upon. The possible use of labyrinths in and around the home is only limited by the homeowner's imagination.

Spirit Spots," by Hilary Rice and a Wall Hanging, by Lorraine Johnson-Brotsky

*Go to page 34 or 119*

Below are photographs of two portable needlework finger labyrinths I designed and stitched: one needlepoint, the other crewel. Instructions for making them follow, at the end of this chapter.

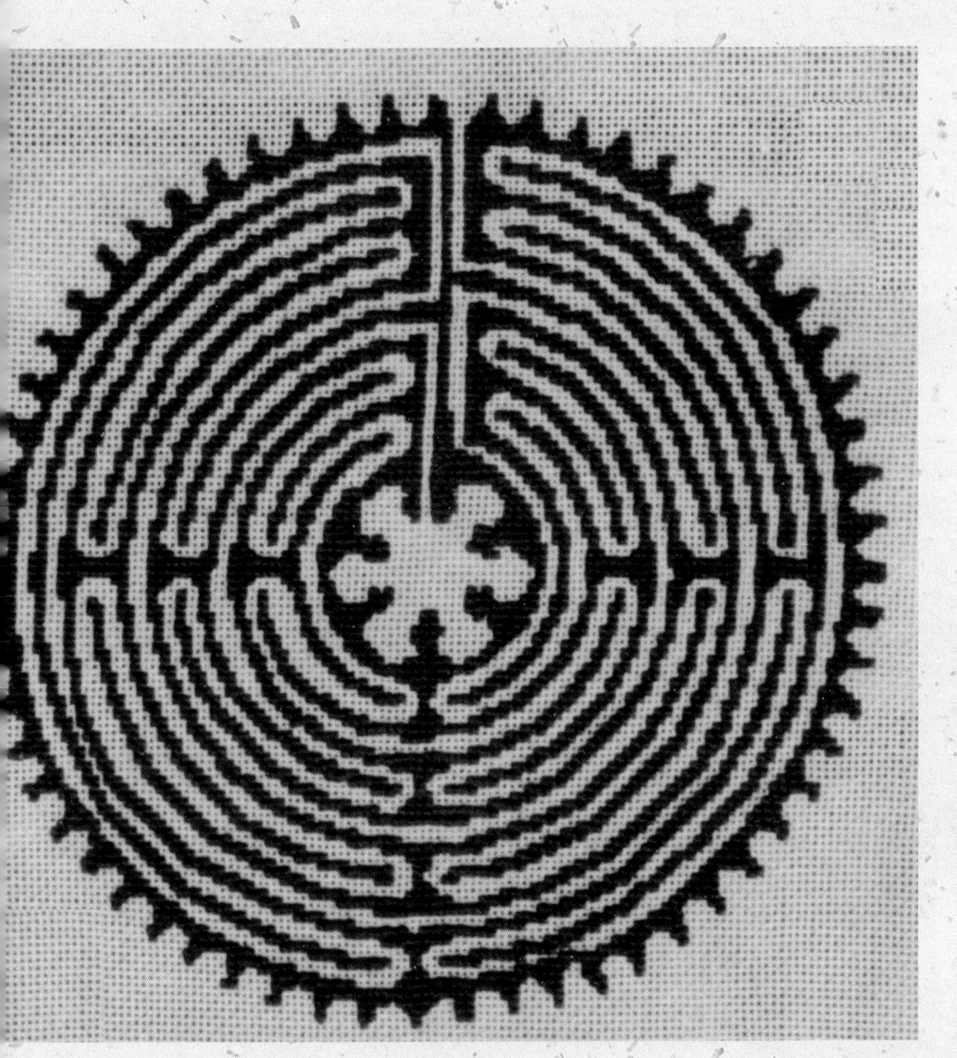

A Portable Needlepoint Cross-Stich Labyrinth

A Portable Crewel Labyrinth

*Go to page 94 or 119*

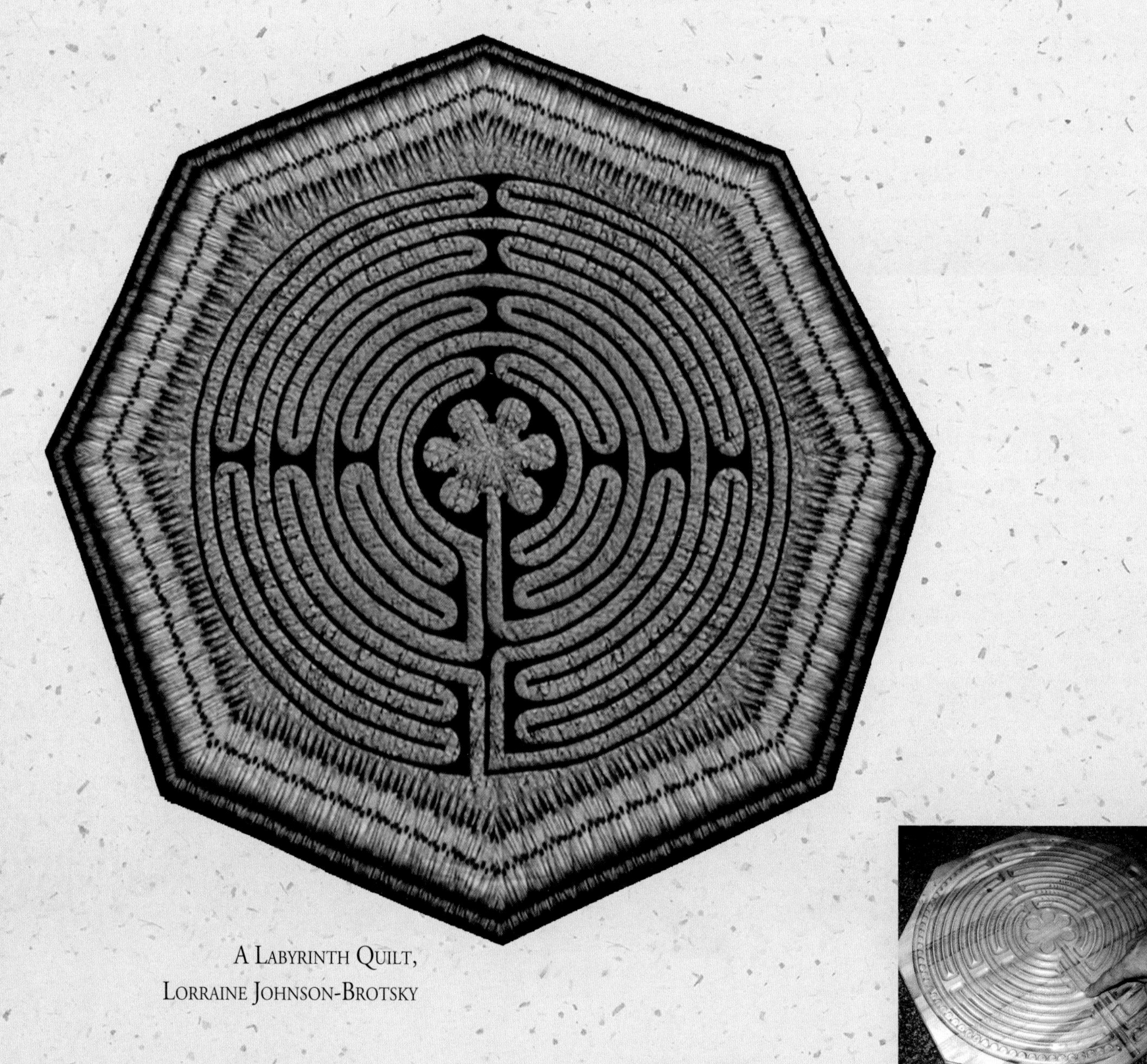

A Labyrinth Quilt,
Lorraine Johnson-Brotsky

A Carved Finger Labyrinth,
Gilbert Giesbrecht

*Go to page 97 or 111*

## THE MODERN CHRISTIAN LABYRINTH

Lauren Artress was changed by her experience of the labyrinth at Chartres Cathedral, changed in ways that she would not have predicted. When she returned to her work at Grace Cathedral in San Francisco, she began to foster the use of the labyrinth as a spiritual tool. Grace Cathedral and Dr. Artress have become the leading authorities on the use of the Chartres-style labyrinth in the Christian context.

---

Dr. Artress, basing her ideas on the work of Keith Critchlow, has done a thorough analysis of the sacred geometry of this type of labyrinth. At its core is the rose, which is a symbol of both Mary and Jesus. Buried within the labyrinth are the shapes of ten, two-bladed axe heads. Artress calls them "labrys," relating them to the Cretan double-headed axe. You will notice that these axe heads are the major turning points. Around the outside are 112 partial circles bitten out of the edge. These she calls "lunations" suggesting that they are, in some unspecified way, connected to the lunar cycle. There would be 114, but two are taken out because of the entrance. Artress says that the Chartres-style labyrinth is built on a 13-pointed star, the basis for the seed kit sold through Veriditas for making a Chartres-style labyrinth.

Artress argues that the rose, the labrys, the lunations, indeed, the entire sacred geometry of the labyrinth, represent the feminine face of God. For centuries, passages of scripture that contain feminine images or language for God – *El Shaddai* (God on

THE ROSE

LABRYS

LUNATIONS

*Go to page 80 or 100*

high) and Isaiah's phrase "in pain have I borne you" – were misinterpreted or simply ignored. Today many Christian denominations are struggling to restore a balance between the God of power and might, and the God of compassion and nurture. Feminist theology, in particular, challenges Christians to recognize God not just, or even *primarily,* as Father, but equally as Mother. Artress believes that the labyrinth is a tool for putting us in touch with this feminine face of the divine. Of course, this sense of God as nurturing Mother was never completely suppressed. It runs like an Ariadne's thread through the writings of the mystics. But in our time it has become a concern for ordinary Christians and the labyrinth can be one tool on the path to balance and wholeness.

All churches are struggling with their relationships with other faiths. Some, following old traditions, see their task as converting people to their own religion. But others try to walk a difficult path by honoring and respecting the faiths of others, while vigorously and faithfully living their own faith. For these people, the labyrinth provides a God-sent opportunity. Here is an unthreatening tool, which most religions share in one form or another; here is a door to significant dialogue and mutual learning; here is a ritual we can celebrate together, without compromising anyone's faith.

Labyrinths have spread very quickly to churches and retreat centers throughout North America and Europe and other parts of the world. Today almost anyone can find a beautiful labyrinth within a convenient distance. For example, about an hour's drive west of my home, I can walk a birch log Hopi labyrinth at a Native Roman Catholic center. An hour and a half drive the other way, a magnificent full-size Chartres-style labyrinth overlooking Lake Nippissing graces the lawn of a convent. Both of these labyrinths are open to the public at any reasonable time.

Labyrinths span Canada, from St. Andrew's United Church, in Halifax, to White Rock United Church, in Vancouver. Almost all mainline denominations have at least some labyrinths, as do groups such as the Unitarians. Labyrinths have also spread to schools and hospitals and, in a few places, to housing complexes. There is even a Cretan labyrinth for the use of inmates only in the yard of the jail in Brockville, Ontario. At the same time, the old cathedral labyrinths of Europe are beginning to be held in new regard. New rituals are being created for these labyrinths and old rituals are being restored. Some labyrinths that had been neglected in the enthusiasm of earlier religious reforms have been restored; new labyrinths have been created for cathedrals that had never had them. The world of spirituality has come a long way since I clambered over chairs at Chartres in 1989.

We have no real way of knowing how many tens of thousands, perhaps hundreds of thousands, of walkers have found comfort, strength, and spirit on the labyrinth. And, in fairness, we have no way of knowing how many have been disappointed. Yet the vast majority of people witness that they have found their experience of the labyrinth calming, at the very least. And many, of course, have found something much deeper and richer still.

*Go to page 100 or 101*

## THE LABYRINTH AND SIMPLICITY

My experience of the labyrinth changes, or is different, each time I walk it. Sometimes I find it energizing; more often I find it calming. Sometimes I experience it as dramatic; more often as mildly pleasant. But I have never had a bad or even disappointing experience with the labyrinth.

More and more, the most important gift that the labyrinth gives me is the promise of simplicity. We live in a confusing, complex, uncertain world. Our life circumstances constantly force us to make important decisions with limited knowledge. Symbolically speaking, life is a maze. Yet, in the labyrinth, life is simple. All I need to do is trust and I will find my center and return to the world. For me, the labyrinth symbolizes simple faith. All I need to do is trust the Path, and, as Julian of Norwich wrote, "All will be well, and all will be well, and all manner of thing will be well."

*Go to page 100 or 101*

## EXPERIENCE

A finger labyrinth is extremely versatile. It is readily portable and can be used anywhere, anytime. Since it primarily involves an experience of touch, the finger labyrinth can be used in the dark, or with closed eyes, or even by visually challenged persons.

A finger labyrinth can be created from almost any rigid material. It can be carved in wood with a router, for example, or formed in clay. The two examples below reflect my own interest in stitchery, but you can use your imagination. The photograph on page 111 shows a needlepoint finger labyrinth that I designed especially for this book (see pattern on page 119). Don't expect that such a labyrinth will follow all the curves perfectly. Part of the beauty of needlepoint is the way in which the roughly textured wool stitches retain their own character, even while simulating the shape of the pattern.

To make a needlepoint labyrinth you will need a piece of #10 or #12 white mono canvas (10 or 12 stitches to the inch) at least 16" square, a set of 14" stretcher bars (12" for #12), 10 skeins of tapestry wool, a #18 tapestry needle, and a small sharp pair of scissors. All of this will be available from any needlework shop. I have used green wool because I had a lot left over from another project. Navy wool would be nice, or bright red, or even white (white wool stitches on white canvas would be very dramatic). You can either mount the needlepoint on the stretcher bars and then stitch it, or stitch it first and then mount it. In either case, be sure that it is mounted very tightly. It is much harder to follow the labyrinth if the canvas sags.

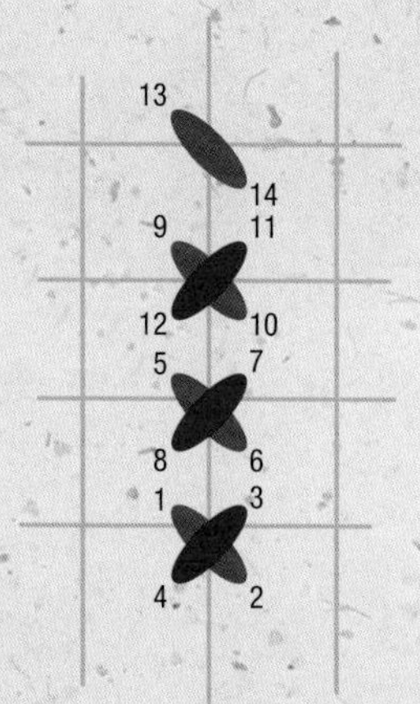


THE CROSS-STITCH

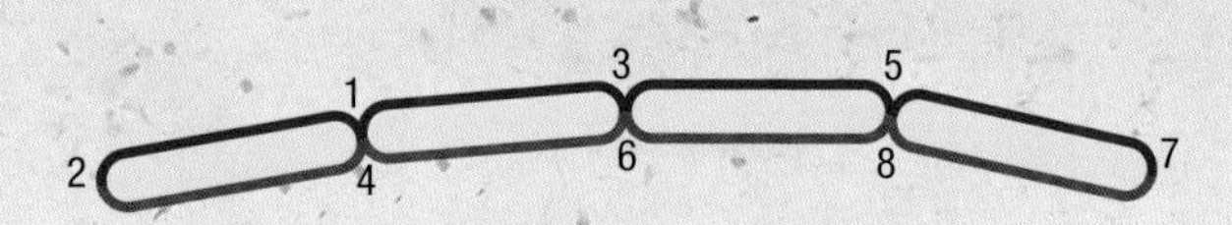


THE BACKSTITCH

*Go to page 102 or 115*

There are many needlepoint stitches that would work for this pattern. I recommend the cross-stitch because it gives a deeper texture for the finger to touch. Use 18" lengths of wool. Bring the wool through from the back of the canvas. Hold a 1" tail of the wool in place on the back with your left hand. As you start stitching, cover this tail and it will anchor your wool solidly. To end a strand, run a 1" tail back under your stitching and clip it off. From now on, you can begin a strand by running all but a 1" tail through the wool already stitched. The result will be well-anchored wool and also a neat back, which is important in a piece like this where only part of the canvas is covered. Any tag ends would show through.

To do the actual stitching, bring the strand of wool up from the back at 1, and go back down at 2 and pull it snug. Now come back up at 3 and down at 4. This time when you pull it snug, it will form a thick cross-stitch. Repeat with 5, 6, 7, and 8. Note that all the top stitches should lie in the same diagonal direction. See the pattern for the cross-stich on page 116. Because of the irregularity of the pattern, you cannot always work in a horizontal line, so you have to improvise a bit as you go.

For a smaller finger labyrinth, you could make one in crewel using the seven-ringed Cretan labyrinth (see the photograph on page 111). For this you will need an 8" x 8" piece of fabric, 2 skeins of embroidery floss, a set of 6" stretcher bars, a needle, and small sharp scissors. Again, these should be available from any needlework shop. Mount the fabric on the stretcher bars pulling it very tightly. Copy the pattern on page 118, shown in actual size, on the fabric using a waterproof pen, and centering it.

Begin at one of the ends of the labyrinth walls; make a knot in the tail of your floss and pull it through from the back. Now backstitch (see the pattern on page 116) with stitches short enough to follow the curves completely, covering the lines with backstitching.

Next, start over at the beginning and stitch French knots all along the backstitching. Again, begin with a knotted strand of floss coming from the back of the material and following the stitch pattern below. Bring the needle up from the back; wrap the point tightly with the floss at least five times; then go back down through the material, pulling snugly to form a neat knot. Cover all the backstitching with French knots. This takes a long time, but the French knots create the texture that allows this be used as a finger labyrinth.

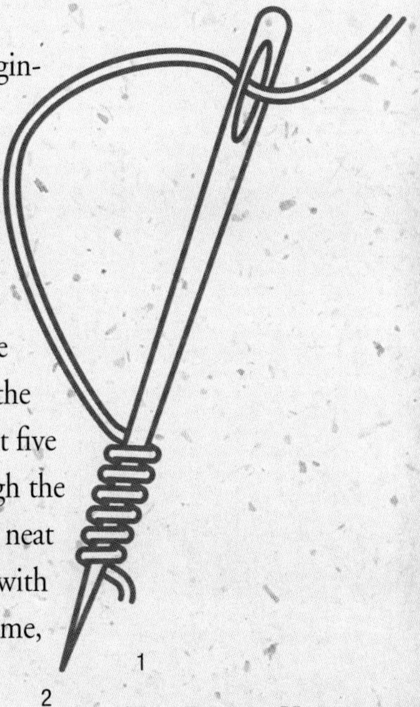

1
2
The French Knot

I have used variegated floss for an interesting effect, but you can use whatever colors appeal to you. One advantage of the crewel labyrinth is the ability to have almost any color background you want, according to the material you choose.

*Go to page 105 or 107*

Pattern for Crewel Finger Labyrinth

*Go to page 61 or 107*

PATTERN FOR A NEEDLEPOINT FINGER LABYRINTH
BASED ON THE CHARTRES LABYRINTH

*Go to page 112 or 117*

***The sound of the path 5.*** The modern use of the Christian labyrinth seems naturally to cry out for accompanying choral music, though this may merely reflect my own bias. Almost any sacred choral music would be appropriate, but I suppose a purist might opt for some of the great modern choral music – John Rutter's *Requiem,* for example; or just about anything by John Tavener.

As you trace or walk the labyrinth, focus on some of the themes that have interested modern Christian proponents of the labyrinth: interfaith spirituality, the journey of faith, the role of Mary and feminine spirituality, healing, transformation, and spiritual maturity.

Does the labyrinth present you with new insights as you focus on these in turn? If so, can you state clearly what you have learned? Has this chapter added anything to your understanding of Christian spirituality? How is the labyrinth Christian?

Try walking the labyrinth while focusing on the simplicity of the path. Do you find comfort or mystery or both in doing this?

In the previous chapter, you were given an opportunity to play with this book as a maze. Now you can play with it as a labyrinth. One way to think of your experience in a labyrinth is to focus on how it took you deep within yourself and then brought you back out into the real world. You might like to think now about whether this book has done this for you. Are there ways in which this book has taken you deep within yourself? What new insights did you find there? What was it like coming back into the ordinary world? Has the world been changed in any way by your journey into the labyrinth?

LABYRINTH AT NIGHT, ATLANTA, GA

*Go to page 97, 113 or 121*

# Selected Resources

## EASY-TO-FIND RESOURCES

**Artress, Dr. Lauren.**

*Walking a Sacred Path: Rediscovering the Labyrinth as a Sacred Tool.*

New York: Riverhead Books, 1995.

This is the book that reintroduced the labyrinth as a spiritual tool. It is full of wisdom and wonder. If you love the labyrinth, it belongs on your bookshelf.

**Fisher, Adrian and Howard Loxton.**

*Secrets of the Maze: An Interactive Guide to the World's Most Amazing Mazes.*

Hauppauge, New York: Barron's, 1997.

Over the years Adrian Fisher, Great Britain's foremost maze designer, has co-authored a number of books. The latest and best is a collection of the most important historic and modern mazes. The accompanying information is invaluable. My only regret is that the authors have seen fit to layer other puzzles over most of the mazes to cater, I suppose, to the current taste for more difficult mazes.

**Hohmuth, Jurgen.**

*Labyrinths and Mazes.*

New York: Prestal, 2003.

This expensive coffee table book will impress your friends. It is full of beautiful photographs and has chapters elegantly written by a who's who of European maze and labyrinth authorities. It does not, however, offer anything in the way of interactive experience.

**Manson, Christopher.**

*Maze: Solve the World's Most Challenging Puzzle.*

New York: Holt, Rinehart and Winston, 1985.

The $10,000 prize for solving this book maze was collected over 15 years ago, but the book is still in print and is still a pleasure to play with.

*Go to page 122 or 124*

**Matthews, W. H.**

*Mazes and Labyrinths: Their History and Development.*

New York: Dover Publications, 1970 (originally published in 1922).

Still in print after 83 years, this is the standard that the rest of us try vainly to match.

**Sands, Helen Raphael.**

*The Healing Labyrinth: Finding your Path to Inner Peace.*

Hauppauge, New York: Barron's, 2001.

Beautifully illustrated, this is the most thoughtful and insightful book presenting a New Age understanding of the labyrinth.

**Saward, Jeff.**

*Labyrinths and Mazes: A Complete Guide to Magical Paths of the World..*

New York: Lark Books, 2003.

This chronological encyclopedia of sacred paths is unique in that it includes many maps and an extensive bibliography.

**Wright, Craig.**

*The Maze and the Warrior.*

Cambridge, Massachusetts: Harvard University Press, 2004.

This is an original and challenging interpretation of the medieval labyrinth, by an academic musicologist. The copies of medieval art are stunning. Even I could manage the music, and the insights are well worth the effort.

## DIFFICULT-TO-FIND RESOURCES

*Time spent exploring used bookstores, used computer game stores, remainder tables and eBay® can result in surprising finds. Here are a few books and things I would recommend, which are no longer in print.*

### *Books*

**Bord, Janet.**

*Mazes and Labyrinths of the World.*

New York: E. P. Dutton, 1976. Out of print.

This is a classic, full of beautiful illustrations and fascinating information, by a well-known British folklorist.

**Travers, P. L.**

*What the Bee Knows: Reflections on Myth, Symbol, and Story.*

Wellingborough, Northamptonshire, U.K.: The Aquarian Press, 1989. Out of print.

This is my "desert island" choice. If I could have only one thing to read about labyrinths and mazes, it would be the chapter called "Walking the Maze at Chartres," from this book. It is just six pages out of 303, but Travers brings back every feeling of my experience of the Chartres labyrinth, only I could

*Go to page 123 or 124*

never say it as well. When it comes to describing the labyrinth, the creator of Mary Poppins is "practically perfect in every way."

**Saward, Jeff.**

*Magical Paths: Mazes and Labyrinths in the 21st Century.*

London, U. K.: Mitchell Beazley, 2002.

This book is not available in North America but I found a single copy on a remainder table in a mall in North Bay, Ontario. So there's hope for finding almost anything! The great strength of this book is its striking photographs of modern mazes and labyrinths including the amazing path brushed by Chris Parsons into dew-laden grass.

### *Magazine*

*Notre-Dame de Chartres.*

Mars 1984, No 58.

I have no idea if this publication is still available, but it contains a wealth of information on cathedral labyrinths. It also has six wonderful pictures of the Chartres labyrinth, some from angles not available to tourists like me. You will find it an invaluable resource whether or not you are able to read French.

### *CD-ROM*

*MAZE.*

Helsingborg, Sweden: Dragonfire Research, 1995. Out of circulation.

This CD-ROM is getting quite out of date; it's terribly Eurocentric; it's very limited in its analysis. Yet the moment you put it into your computer, you'll know that you have a treasure. You can see drawings of actual mazes from two different angles: from above in plan, and from the side as hedge mazes. You can generate lots of paper mazes for children. But most of all, you get a quite effective three-dimensional simulation of a good number of real mazes. Just one word of warning: turn the sound off. The music that accompanies the simulation is unbelievably annoying.

GARDEN LABYRINTH, BUHL, IDAHO

*Go to page 121 or 124*

# INTERNET RESOURCES

*As everyone is aware, the Internet must be used selectively, but here are a few resources that I have found helpful in different ways.*

www.labyrinthina.com/path.htm

This is one of the best of the New Age labyrinth sites. It also includes information on making a walking labyrinth for under $10.00. My best effort so far is just under $50.00.

OSWEGO, ILLINOIS

www.labyrinthos.net/homepage.htm

Jeff and Kimberly Saward provide information and professional services for labyrinth and maze enthusiasts through their Labyrinth Resource Centre. Access to *CAERDROIA*, the annual labyrinth journal is also found here.

www.labyrinthsociety.org

This is the source for information about the online labyrinth organization and its annual meeting. Kimberly Saward is the president.

www.labyrinth-toronto.ca

You will find access here to a great deal of useful information including a current listing for all registered labyrinth sites and all registered labyrinth facilitators in Ontario. The same information for Alberta is available through www.ualberta.ca . And from there it is possible to access Manitoba's labyrinth network. Other provinces do not currently have labyrinth registries.

www.mymaze.de/home_e.htm

The German site is in English and includes lots of examples of labyrinths not included in this book or in English language resources generally.

www.veriditas.net

This outstanding site developed by Lauren Artress and her colleagues includes excellent resources for purchase and the World Wide Labyrinth Locator.

*Go to page 122 or 123*

# Maze Solutions

*Three-dimensional Maze p. 95*

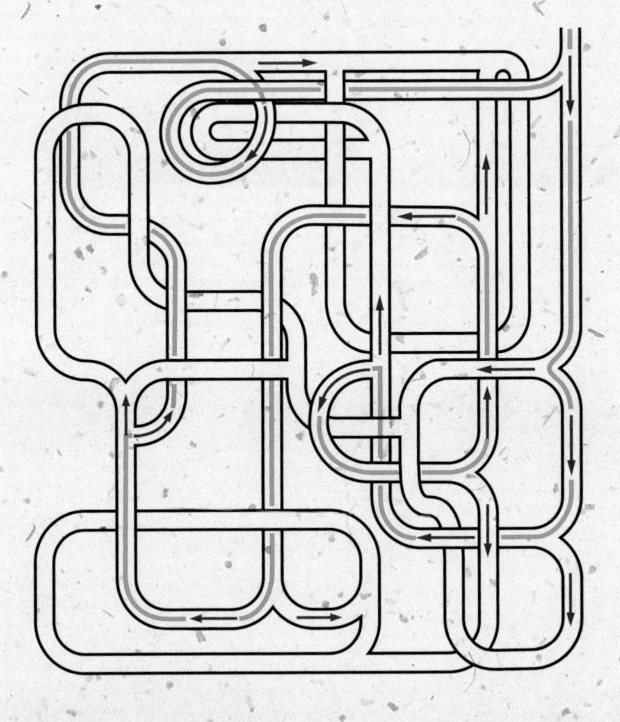

*Word Maze p. 97*

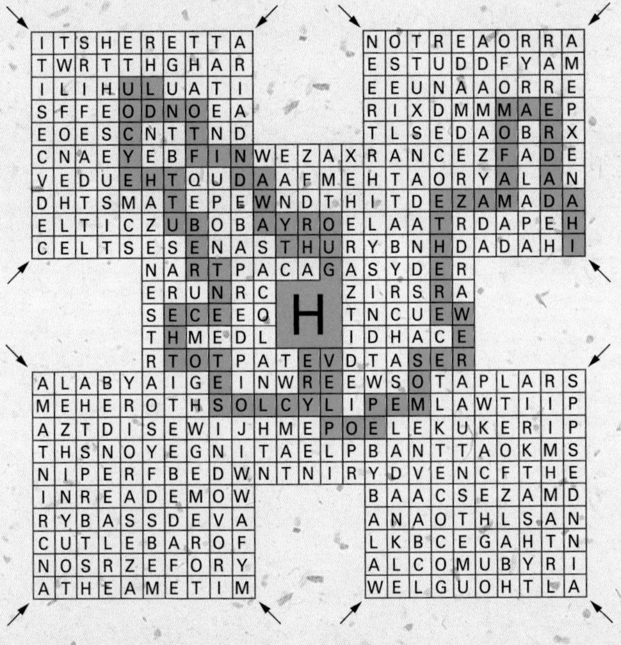

"I had a dream of a maze. There were some people very close to the centre but they could not find a way through."

REV. DR. ROBERT RUNCIE,
ARCHBISHOP OF CANTERBURY

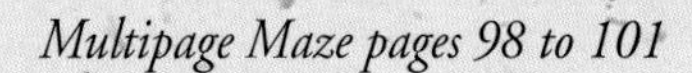

*Multipage Maze pages 98 to 101*

*Book Maze*

96 → 41 → 39 → 70 → 110 → 34 → 65 → 30 → 31 → 90 → 118 → 61 → 23 → 58 → 85 → 56 → 17 → 103 → 120 → 113 → 80 → 15 → 11 → 9 → 46 → 77

# Credits

**Editor:** Michael Schwartzentruber
**Concept for "The Spirituality Of" series:** Northstone Team
**Cover and interior design:** Margaret Kyle
**Proofreader:** Dianne Greenslade

NORTHSTONE PUBLISHING is an imprint of WOOD LAKE BOOKS, INC.
Wood Lake Books acknowledges the financial support of the Government of Canada, through the Book Publishing Industry Development Program (BPIDP) for its publishing activities.

WOOD LAKE BOOKS is an employee-owned company, committed to caring for the environment and all creation. Wood Lake Books recycles, reuses, and encourages readers to do the same. Resources are printed on recycled paper and more environmentally friendly groundwood papers (newsprint), whenever possible. The trees used are replaced through donations to the Scoutrees For Canada Program. A percentage of all profit is donated to charitable organizations.



Published by Northstone Publishing
an imprint of WOOD LAKE BOOKS, INC.
9025 Jim Bailey Road, Kelowna, BC, Canada, V4V 1R2
250.766.2778
www.northstone.com

**Line Illustrations**: Verena Velten

**Photographs (Copyright © of the following. Used with permission):**
Joyce DeMeester, Kelowna, BC, Canada
cover and page 3, hedge maze, Salmon Arm, BC

Adrian Fisher, Adrian Fisher Mazes Ltd , www.mazemaker.com
page 6: herb garden
page 8, 19: hedge maze, Longleat, Wiltshire, UK
page 21: Parham, Sussex, UK
page 24: hedge water maze
page 46, 66, 84: mirror maze, Longleat, Wiltshire, UK
page 67: maize maze; hedge maze, Leeds Castle, Leeds, UK
page 87: fence or panel maze, Holywell Bay, Newquay, Cornwell, UK
page 88: Planet maze, East Tawas, Michigan, USA
page 90: maize maze
page 91: Edinburgh maze, UK

Michael Fox, www.knowth.com
page 2: entrance stone, Newgrange, UK
page 29: labyrinth carved on the wall of15th-century church, Rathmore, UK
page 74: winter soltice sunshine, Newgrange, UK
page 102: standing stone, Newgrange, UK

Gilbert Giesbrecht, Carbon, AB, Canada
page 112: carved finger labyrinth designed and created by Gilbert Giesbrecht, Box 152 Carbon, Alberta, Canada, T0M 0L0, gilbertg@telusplanet.net

Lois Huey Heck, Northstone Publishing, Kelowna, BC, Canada
cover and page 3: labyrinth at Naramata Centre, BC

Lorraine Johnson-Brotsky, Vernon, BC, Canada
page 110: wall hanging or floor cloth painted in stages over four weeks during Lent by Lorraine Johnson-Brotsky. Each stage being a portion of the path with the color lightening as it gets closer to the center. Acrylic on canvas, 96" x 96"
page 112: "To quilt the labyrinth is a creative journey. To walk the labyrinth is a spiritual journey." Labyrinth art quilt by Lorraine Johnson-Brotsky, based on the Chartres labyrinth. Machine pieced and piped and hand quilted, 64" x 64"

Phillip Charles Lucas , Stetson University, DeLand, FL, USA
page 70, 71: Rocky Valley labyrinth, Tintagel Village, Cornwall, UK

Gailand MacQueen, Sudbury, ON, Canada
page 33: Minoan Bull Fresco, Crete
page 72: Saffron Walden labyrinth, Essex, UK
page 79: dancing the labyrinth
page 96: Hedge Garden
page 107: Sisters of St. Joseph Mother House, North Bay, ON
page 111: portable needlepoint cross-stitch and portable crewel labyrinth

www.photos.com
page 4 and 5: stone doorways
page 14, 17, 53, 93
page 20: freeway maze
page 45: wooden pathway
page 59: hedge maze
page 64: hedge maze
page 65: boy drawing a maze
page 74: rose window, Chartres Cathedral
page 85: computer maze
page 94: "metaphor of life" maze

Hilary Rice, Invermere, BC, Canada
page 110: "Spirit Spots" – hand dyed, printed, stitched and beaded by fiber artist Hilary Rice of M. E. Studios, ricicles@telus.net. The "cross labyrinth" is a design created by Hilary Rice.

Eva Schwartzentruber
page 18: carved labyrinth, Lucca, Italy

Jeff Saward/Labyrinthos, www.labyrinthos.net
page 1: petroglyph, Arroyo Hondo, New Mexico
page 8: Stardreaming, New Mexico
page 12: Philo, California
page 15: Chartres replica on canvas
page 24: ball-bearing labyrinth
page 25: ceramic labyrinth
page 30: Neolithic spirals
page 32: Otfrid Labyrinth
page 34: Cretan coins
page 35: a Roman labyrinth mosaic
page 36: Scandinavian stone labyrinth, Tisvildeleje, Denmark
page 37: Tohono O'odham plaque, Native American labyrinth
page 38: Saffron Walden labyrinth, Essex, UK
page 39: Maypole, Tulstrup, Denmark
page 41, 73: Chartres Cathedral, France
page 54: hedge maze, New Harmony, Indiana, USA
page 68: Rocky Valley labyrinth, Tintagel Village, Cornwall, UK
page 105: Glastonbury Tor, Glastonbury, Isle of Avalon, UK
page 108: World Peace canvas labyrinth
page 109: Santa Rosa canvas labyrinth
page 115: labyrinth, Hilton, Cambridgeshire, UK
page 120: labyrinth at night, Atlanta, GA
page 123: garden labyrinth, Buhl, Idaho, USA
page 124: Oswego, Illinois, USA
page 128: Tohono O'odham pottery